NASHVILLE
PREDATORS

JUSTIN B. BRADFORD

NASHVILLE PREDATORS

THE MAKING OF SMASHVILLE

Foreword by
PETE WEBER

THE
History
PRESS

Published by The History Press
Charleston, SC
www.historypress.net

First published 2015

Manufactured in the United States

ISBN 978.1.62619.850.0

Library of Congress Control Number: 2015947679

To the Predators fans who have been there through it all, this one is for you. And for all of you newer fans, I hope you're able to learn something great about the team you love.

To all of you surprised that a half Asian with the last name Bradford wrote a hockey book, hi.

To my mom and dad, thank you.

CONTENTS

FOREWORD

It's very difficult for me to believe that the Predators have been around for so long. It's been seventeen years as of this writing, and it has been some ride.

I remember being on the World Wide Web in the spring of 1997 and reading that the NHL was ready to conditionally award expansion franchises to Nashville, Atlanta, Columbus and Minnesota. This would bring hockey back to Atlanta, where the Flames' owners simply got from Calgary too good a deal to refuse in 1980, and to Minnesota, where ownership had run into financial difficulties and finally moved to Dallas in 1993. However, Nashville and Columbus represented incursions into markets that had familiarity with the minor-league version of the sport.

It all seems like a whirlwind now. The Thrashers moved from Atlanta to Winnipeg in 2011. Columbus has proved to be an outstanding hockey market. Minnesota was almost instantaneously a hit, playing in St. Paul rather than Bloomington. But Nashville has been a special story.

From a standing ovation for the opening faceoff on October 10, 1998, you could tell this city had a particular flair. There were maybe 250 registered amateur hockey players and only one ice surface outside of what is now Bridgestone Arena. Now, more than 2,000 amateurs are playing the game on six rinks in Middle Tennessee, and the team is producing sellout after sellout.

This wasn't easily accomplished. The Predators have survived two lockouts, one of which cost them a whole season immediately after making the playoffs. In 2007, it appeared the team might be suddenly sold and moved out of town, becoming just a nine-year blip on the Nashville sports scene. Thankfully, the team was rescued by local ownership. Justin Bradford has talked to so many involved with the story and lays it all out for you here. If I hadn't lived it, I might not believe it myself!

PETE WEBER
Voice of the Nashville Predators

ACKNOWLEDGEMENTS

I would like to express my sincerest gratitude to all who were able to make this book possible. First and foremost, thank you to God for blessing me with such wonderful opportunities in my life. I wouldn't be here without His grace.

Thank you to my parents, Jerry and Vivien, for all of their support. Through anything, they have always been there for me. My family and extended family have always been so supportive, and I wouldn't be the man I am today without them.

Without Jules Festa, I would never have received the opportunity to write for The History Press. Thank you to her and to The History Press for this wonderful opportunity.

The Nashville Predators were so supportive throughout this entire process. They put me in touch with alumni and former executives of the organization. A tremendous thank-you to Sean Henry, Gerry Helper, Alexis Witman, Thomas Willis and Brooks Bratten for their help. And to Kayla Evans, your assistance with quotes will not be forgotten.

Thank you to all of the former players and coaches who gave me the time of day to speak with them about this project. They are the ones who made this book possible.

Without a little encouragement from my friends in 303, my love of writing never would have been discovered. Thank you.

I can't even imagine doing this without the support from my crew at Penalty Box Radio. Ben Butzbach and Glynne Blackwell, you've been there since the start. Thank you! We've grown something special from the ground up, and you've helped make it all possible.

Lastly, to Predators fans: your words of encouragement and congratulations when this whole process started meant the world to me. Your support deserves my heartfelt thanks.

1
LAYING THE FOUNDATION

The history of hockey in Nashville did not begin with the Nashville Predators. The groundwork for creating a hockey-crazed fan base began in the 1960s and built from there. Nashville has been home to multiple minor-league franchises over the years, including the Dixie Flyers, the South Stars, the Knights, the Nighthawks and the Ice Flyers. Each generation had a team to call its own that introduced it to the game.

Fast-forward to 1997, and a new team would begin to lay the foundation for new hockey fans for generations to come.

In the mid-1990s, as Metropolitan Nashville–Davidson County continued to grow, the opportunity for professional sports franchises came with it. With the Bridgestone Arena (formerly Nashville Arena) opening in 1996, a major tenant was needed to fill it. There were attempts to bring in a National Basketball Association franchise, as well as heavy rumors of a National Hockey League team relocating to Nashville. After both attempts did not come to fruition, the original owner of the Nashville Predators, Craig Leipold, decided to go the route of expansion. The process began in January 1997, and on June 25, 1997, the city of Nashville was awarded an NHL franchise.

"Back in the late '90s, I was really concentrating on buying an NBA team," said Leipold.

> *I talked to a number of owners and made a few offers, but nothing got a ton of traction. I came down to Nashville around 1996, and I was on the board of the Levy organization, which is a concession company, and they*

Former Nashville mayor and Tennessee governor Phil Bredesen and his wife, Andrea Conte. *Don Olea Photography*.

were having a meeting with Gaylord in Nashville. So I leave Wisconsin, where it's cold and snowy and sleeting and raining, and I am landing in Nashville in April and the weather is spectacular. It is the most phenomenal day with no humidity, in the low seventies, and they are building this arena. I go, "Wow, what is going to go in there?" and in the course of the next twenty-four hours I e-mailed all the people at Gaylord at the meeting, and we spent a lot of time talking about the arena and what sport was going to go in there. They were actively trying to recruit an owner to buy an NBA or NHL team and put it in the new arena that would be completed in the next twelve months.

So, that was the genesis of it all, and all of a sudden Nashville became a great opportunity. I flew down about two weeks later to meet with the mayor of Nashville, who was Phil Bredesen, and developed a really strong relationship with Mayor Bredesen. He was a very progressive advocate for downtown Nashville, and so the two of us went to visit the NBA office and the NHL office, and we told them that we were interested in putting a pro team in the downtown Nashville arena. Both leagues were very interested in Nashville, and so that was the beginning of getting a team to either move, or if it was an expansion franchise, to have the league award the city an expansion franchise.

Long story short, it became the NHL, and we were in competition with a number of cities when the NHL said they were going to initiate an expansion franchise. We were in competition with Canadian cities, other U.S. cities and, fortunately, we were awarded one of the franchises. That is kind of how it all started. It obviously took a lot of time and effort, and a lot of people helped. It took about twelve months; we were busy selling the city of why Nashville would be a good market.

With Nashville being added as an expansion franchise, three other NHL clubs would also be added over the next three seasons: the Atlanta Thrashers, the Minnesota Wild and the Columbus Blue Jackets. For NHL commissioner Gary Bettman, Nashville presented a good opportunity for growing the sport.

"We were intrigued by the possibility of being in a city like Nashville that was known for entertainment, for hospitality and was a good sports town but didn't really have much in the way of professional sports," Bettman said, "and we thought based on the proposed ownership, the fact that there was a beautiful arena, empty, this might be a good opportunity for NHL hockey."

Around the same time, the National Football League was beginning to make its presence known in Nashville. Following the 1996 NFL season, the

Houston Oilers announced that they would be moving to Nashville. The team, however, would not become known as the Tennessee Titans until it moved into its new stadium, slated to open for the 1999 NFL season.

So just like that, the city of Nashville gained two professional sports team in the span of two years. While the Predators would not hit the ice until the 1998 season, there was plenty of work to do to begin building the team: hiring a general manager, coaching staff and administrators, as well as answering the all-important question of what the team would be called and creating its logo. Not only that, but now the work of selling the people of Nashville on becoming major supporters of an NHL club had to begin. Yes, hockey had some roots in the city, but with the NHL comes a major investment.

"One of the real issues we had with Nashville was: would they embrace the game of hockey?" said Craig Leipold.

> *Nashville was dying to get a professional sport because the Titans were not in Nashville. We wanted to be the first professional sports team. What really excited me about Nashville was the progressive, ambitious political environment and a very vibrant community with a large corporate base, the music industry, the healthcare industry, all the banking, the energy; it is a corporate base that has leadership that was willing to get involved in something that would help the city. They became real advocates in helping us to get the word out about season tickets, so in the beginning it was not so much that we were selling hockey; we were selling Nashville becoming a big city.*
>
> *It is time that Nashville was no longer considered a second-tier city. It was about making Nashville into a big market. That is really what drove it in the beginning, and it really worked out that way; we went to the music community, and the stars helped us get the word out and [were] always available when we had events or some kind of season ticket sales event. They would come out and sing, and we would get a lot of people out there and they would buy tickets.*

With that in mind, Leipold had to build the team from the ground up. Jack Diller was hired as the first president of the Nashville Predators on July 1, 1997, and David Poile as the first—and currently only—general manager on July 9, 1997.

"The only person I hired was Jack Diller," recalled Leipold.

> *Jack hired David Poile, and David Poile hired Barry Trotz. It was a great partnership between the four of us. We all knew our boundaries and*

respected the other person's boundaries. I would never get involved in hockey operations. David chose his players with Barry. I was very involved with the business operations, which is the sales and marketing side, from the very beginning. When it came to the hockey business, it was all Poile and Trotz. They built this team from the ground up.

We all talked about what kind of team did we want and what kind of team would Nashville be able to respect and be looking for. It would be a hardworking team giving 110 percent every single night. You didn't have the flashy superstars and really fill this team for the long haul instead of a flash-in-the-pan team, and that is how we did it.

The first parts of administration were now in place. Now came the task of building a team. General manager David Poile saw coming to the Predators as a good opportunity. After spending fifteen years with the Washington Capitals and five years before that with the Flames, Poile was now at the helm of an expansion franchise—a challenge, but one that he wanted.

"I did think it was a fantastic opportunity. I had another chance to be with another established club, but I thought the ultimate experience would be to start something from the ground floor," said Poile.

You work for good or for bad—you're going to have your fingerprints on everything that goes, from helping to design the dressing room to working on the layout of the office to choosing the name of the franchise, the color of the uniforms and getting into specific things like hiring out your scouting stuff and hiring your coaches, picking out where your farm club is going to be and develop a direction, specifically a philosophy, for your franchise and how it is going to go from expansion franchise into a successful franchise.

Poile's first hire was obviously going to be at the head coach position. It was important to lay the groundwork and hire someone who could gain from the experience, as well as become the face of the franchise while the team continued to build. After speaking with other peers in hockey, Poile came to the conclusion that he wanted to give someone a chance to make an impression. Less than a month after Poile himself was hired, on August 6, 1997, he named Barry Trotz as the first head coach in the history of the franchise.

"When I got the job, I called a couple of my other peers who had been with expansion teams and asked about their experience and what they would do, and they always said the same thing: your team is not going to be very good, and you should hire the most experienced coach you can get to cover up a lot of the problems and mistakes of your franchise," said Poile.

> *I gave it a lot of thought, and what I decided was someone giving me a chance along the way. I got my start with a new club where expectations were low, and I decided I would hire a lot of new scouts, first-time scouts, to give them a chance, and it also went into the coaching part, where Barry Trotz, who[m] I knew from my days in the Washington Capitals and was a very good coach, up and coming with a good track record wherever he's been, and why not give him a chance? That was one of the best decisions I ever made.*

That partnership would last for fifteen years, much longer than anyone thought it would. Having an already established relationship between the general manager and the head coach certainly helped in establishing the franchise. When hired, Trotz was excited for the opportunity but was also aware of the potential challenges.

"David called me, and I had worked with David for a number of years as a minor-league coach and had great success in Portland," said Trotz.

> *He called and asked if he could interview me and said I would be the perfect guy to start the franchise. I was thrilled, and at the same time, it was one of those things when he hung up the phone that I thought, what did I just get myself into? It was pretty scary as an untraditional coach going into an expansion team in an untraditional market—that had really not been done before—so there was a moment I was terrified for a second, and then I took a deep breath and said, "I am ready for this. Let's just go after it."*

Now that the front office was beginning to take shape, the all-important challenge of naming the team was at the helm. Leipold was a huge part of this process. The front office wanted something that related to the area but was also marketable.

"That is one thing I was very involved in—that was all what you were selling. We had to have a good logo, and we had to have a good name," said Leipold.

> *Obviously you are aware of the history of the saber-toothed tiger in the Middle Tennessee market, so we really liked the concept of the saber-toothed tiger. But because it was the Buffalo Sabres, even though their sabre is a sword, we could not use the word sabre in our name. We had to come*

up with another name that would sound like it represented a saber-toothed tiger. I did what anybody else would do: I opened up a dictionary, and how does it describe a saber-toothed tiger? A predator.

It was more of a process than one might think. Everyone in the front office was involved. But once they found the name they wanted, they knew it was the one. Because of the events dominating the news of the era, they wanted to gauge public opinion about the team name. The entire front office, including Trotz, took part in the naming of the team.

"The great thing about the expansion team is that we started from nothing. We dealt with empty bowls, and when I got the job, David offered to take me to the office, and I walked in and it was a big dining room," said Trotz.

We started from scratch, though, and that's the great thing about it, but it was long hours, and you dealt with every aspect of building a team. Everything about coming in as an expansion coach was that you were part of every process—electing the team staff, carpet colors, dressing room swatches. You talk about going to a hockey university; you are part of scouting and management and architecture, just every aspect of the facility.

When they were picking it, they had a logo but no name. I remember how David asked if I had any ideas for a name, and I started going through an old CHL book, and there was a team called the Predators, and I thought Nashville Predators sounded OK. And lo and behold, it became the Predators! I can't take credit for the name because I didn't pick it, but the focus group did. I know that was one we submitted. We had all the goofy names, like the Nashville Cats and the Ice Tigers, and the logo was always the same. We handed it in, and months later it made it through the focus groups, and it seemed to work. I remember my son was young at the time, and he found a dinosaur book, and in it was replica of a saber-toothed tiger.

Leipold went into further detail about the name:

I will tell you that was the name we wanted from day one, but there was something about the name Predator; it was at a time when the sexual predator laws were rolling into effect, and we were very concerned that the community would have a concern about us using the word because of the connotation of the word. We wanted the community to be involved in helping us choose the name, and hopefully the name they would like would be Predator.

Predators mascot Gnash swings from the ceiling. *Don Olea Photography.*

As Barry mentioned, we came up with a number of names, and I will tell you some of the names that were chosen for the contest would be bad names because we wanted Predators to win. We had names like Ice Tigers and the Edge and the Fury, and then we had the Nashville Predators. Sure enough, that won, and so we were able to use the name, and it was the name the city wanted. No one ever had an issue with it or challenged it, and the rest is history. I continue to love the name, and I think the logo is great.

The first generation of the logo was unveiled on September 25, 1997, followed by the Predators name on November 13, 1997.

Preparing to Hit the Ice

As the fall of 1998, the first time the team would hit the ice, approached, now came the part of deciding the direction of the team. As an expansion team, the Predators would enter the draft lottery and participate in the expansion draft. That being said, the team was starting from scratch. It would get the players that other teams did not lock down and protect from the expansion draft.

By getting those types of "expendable" players, the team's identity began to form early on.

"I think the skill level, with all due respect, was not where we could be at a competitive level, so you wanted to get character blue-collar guys," said Poile.

And also, I was looking for assets that might be of interest to other clubs as we moved along with the trade deadline because I fully realized that, with maybe the exception of two or three guys that we could develop on our own or get lucky in expansion draft, until I turned over the entire roster, that was our first generation of Predators. Until I turned over that roster, we're going to stay in the expansion era until we can get into the competitive era.

As of 2015, the Nashville Predators still have never had a number-one overall pick in the NHL draft. In their first draft, they took David Legwand, who played with the team for fourteen full seasons.

"First of all, it was a lottery, which we lost," said Poile on the 1998 draft.

We went from first pick to third. In our mind, Legwand is a top-two player in terms of offense, and wanting to start with a center where all things are equal, but then I had to trade our second-round pick to San Jose at the time to move up from third to second, just to get to Legwand, which is a big price to pay for an expansion team to get their start. But Legwand was rookie of the year, scored fifty goals and looked like he would be a high-end offensive center, and I thought that would be a perfect way to start building the franchise.

The Nashville Predators' first-ever draft pick, David Legwand. *Don Olea Photography.*

Trotz put much of his faith in Poile to help build the right team for Nashville. "David did his homework on expansion teams and had talked to a number of different people, but they all told him to have flexibility and get the younger guys because they're the guys that are going to be there for a year or two, and then you're going to be going by that group of guys into the next group," said Trotz.

As a coach, you're just trying to get the best players possible, so I had to understand what the idea was, and David articulated it quite well that you want to have a couple of veteran guys along the way to stabilize, but they probably aren't the guys who are going to be around when you make the playoffs. The guys who would be around are the young guys who you took in the expansion draft, so I went along, and David had a good plan. We basically broke down every team, what we thought would be the guys available; he did his homework in terms of talking to GMs, and GMs don't want to give you anything, so they were doing certain maneuvers that wouldn't allow them to give up a whole lot.

We tried to stay ahead of the curve and find that next-level player who maybe wasn't at the NHL; if the team was real deep in a certain area, then maybe we could grab one or two of those. We knew the goaltenders—teams would make deals if you took a goaltender, so they wouldn't expose a goaltender in the next draft or something like that. We knew some of those things. We knew we could take a couple players that we could actually just turn into draft choices, so we talked about all those situations, and David was really pretty clear on that. The one thing he said that rung out in a lot of ways was [that] we are probably not going to be very good these next couple of years, so let's think out of the box, try things other people aren't trying because it won't matter. We won't be a cup contender for two years.

Some of the things we thought about were: how are we going to produce goals? Be quick! So we did look at some of the smaller players and said these guys are going to be our best bet to score goals—the small quick guys. We were very aggressive on the fore check; when everybody was trapping, we were sending two guys into the fray on a very continual basis. We took chances on a guy like Kimmo Timonen, who was a small defenseman but a tremendous defenseman, and we got him packaged in with a deal with LA, and he ended up playing the league a long time and was one of the top defensemen for a number of years and had a great career when all of it was said and done. We did take some chances, and a guy like Kimmo Timonen did open the door up for a Brian Rafalski, for a Dan Boyle, for people like that coming into the league. At that point in time, everyone was the size of Darien Hatcher, and we switched it to going a little smaller, and those guys opened a lot of teams' eyes that those smaller guys could play in the league and be very successful.

Kimmo Timonen crashes the net. *Don Olea Photography.*

As the team began to take shape, it was important for the organization to find the right way to market it. In order to be successful, it had to not only ice a good product but also get people in the seats. Nashville, being the "Music City," offered tremendous opportunities from a marketing aspect.

"We had to do very little in order to convince the music community to help us with this," said Leipold.

They were so willing to do whatever it took to be successful. They recognized that Nashville needed this and that the arena was being built for two reasons: one, we needed place for concerts, and two, we needed a professional sports team. Vince Gill was probably the foremost person that was helpful and up front with helping us, and Amy Grant was right there behind Vince.

We did this billboard called Got Tickets, and it was at the time when the Got Milk? campaign was around, and we had this beautiful, iconic country music star like Martina McBride with her front tooth blacked out. The music community could not have been more helpful in getting engaged with whatever they could, and there is no doubt in my mind that a big reason this team is successful in Nashville is the

Vince Gill and Amy Grant perform the national anthem. *Don Olea Photography*.

music community stepped up and said we want to make sure we have a professional sports team in this city.

Getting the music industry involved played a tremendous role in marketing the team. To this day, music makes Nashville Predators games unique. During each intermission, music is heard from a band stage above the Zamboni door.

THE VOICES OF THE PREDATORS

High atop the arena, far from the front office, is where the broadcasting crew can be found. Since the first season, Pete Weber and Terry Crisp have been a part of the Nashville Predators organization. Both instantly became a part of building the team and relaying the message to the fans. Their voices are iconic to anyone who has followed the franchise since 1998—Weber on play-by-play and Crisp on color commentary.

Weber brought with him vast sports knowledge. He spent time with the Los Angeles Kings, Buffalo Sabres and Notre Dame hockey. Weber also has fifteen seasons of experience calling baseball. To this day, he remembers exactly what he was doing the day he heard about Nashville being awarded an NHL franchise:

I was sitting—this is in June of 1997—reading that very high-tech prodigy website and read where the four conditional franchises were being handed out at that point in time. I called my wife, whose parents had settled in Knoxville, so I said, "What do you think about holidays where we only need to drive two and a half hours instead of coming up with these Goliath trips from Buffalo to East Tennessee?" She said, "What are you talking about?" So I explained it to her, and that day I found where Craig Leipold was in Racine, and I FedExed my stuff to him the next day.

So I kept in contact, and then all of a sudden Gerry Helper came here, and I had worked with him with the Sabres in the mid-'80s, then Jack Dillard got hired and on top of all of that I got to show my wares to them because the entry draft was in Buffalo and the expansion draft was in Buffalo in 1998. I got to spend a lot of time with Jack and Craig. Then it was a Fourth of July weekend trip to Knoxville, borrowed my father-in-law's car and drove over here and met with all the wires hanging down from the ceiling in what are the offices now in little cubicles and kept after them, and Gerry kept after them. Preliminary was the first week of August and then final terms agreed upon on August 25, then I was here for the first day of the first training camp on September 12. It was roughly a year and three months' pursuit because I always wanted to be on the launch of a franchise.

Terry Crisp came from a different pedigree than Weber. Having won three Stanley Cups—two as a player and one as a coach—Crisp brought the coach's perspective to the booth. Crisp also brought with him experience with expansion teams, as he was the head coach of the Tampa Bay Lightning from its beginning in 1992 until 1997. Just like Weber, Crisp also had a Nashville connection.

"My first thoughts were, 'NHL…Nashville…no kidding," said Crisp.

Who would have thought? I was offered a job earlier in my career to coach the Nashville Stars as they were then, and unfortunately I was unable to take the job then or I would have been here a lot earlier. Then they announced the fact that Nashville had a team, and it kind of came out of nowhere. There wasn't a lot of hoopla, just suddenly there was a team! Gerry Helper, who had worked with me in Tampa for seven years, was one of the first ones to join the team up here for marketing and

Terry Crisp awards the development camp cup. *Don Olea Photography*.

getting the whole thing going. When he called me, I said, "Really? You want me to come to Nashville?"

I loved Nashville. I had been here for a trip one time, and when we won the cup in 1974 with the Philadelphia Flyers, we made a trip. After we won and everyone asked what we were going to do, we said, "I don't know, we aren't going to Disney World, I can tell you that!" So four of us decided with the wives to come to Nashville; 1974 was our first venture. Then we came back when they started the hockey club here, and the funniest thing is I came here to do one game because they didn't have a TV guy yet. They had the radio guy in place; they didn't have an analyst for their TV, and Pete was already here, so Gerry said come up and do one game. I said I was done and was going to retire and enjoy Florida…so I come up to help.

Couple of days later, Gerry called again and said, "Listen, we've got a double header coming up. We're going to get somebody but if you can just help us out again. Come on!" So I came up and did a couple more games, then they contacted me and said they wanted me to do their TV games. I was getting bored anyway; they said they would fly me in and out and set me up in a hotel, and I said, "You know what? Fly me up and down, me and my wife, I will do it and you don't have to pay me anything for it, I'll do it." So it started! Jack Diller was the president, and we shook hands and he said you can commute if you want! I said, "Tell you what, Jack. I'll sell my house in Florida and move up here!" And he said OK! So I said to my wife, "Guess what, we are moving to Nashville."

That is how quickly it happened, and it was the best move we ever made. Coming here was so unique and original because I was an original St. Louis Blue when they started in 1967. Another start-up in 1972, I was an original Islander. Then, when the Tampa Bay Lightning started up, I was their first coach. So when this one started up, I said, man, I am an original kind of guy! I was lucky to be on the ground floor when they started the franchise.

OPENING NIGHT

Time kept inching closer to October 10, 1998, the date of the franchise's first game. All the work done by Leipold, Diller, Poile, Trotz and the rest of the front office was finally coming to fruition, with their product taking the ice for the first time in the regular season. Trotz's recollection of that night will be longstanding in his memory:

For myself and my family, it was probably no different than a player playing their first NHL game. I was excited, anxious, proud—all of those emotions— and you think about all of those people who helped you get there and mentored you and gave you a place. I know opening night I had my godmother come in; Jack Button, who gave me my first place with the Washington Capitals as a part-time scout, and he got me to training camp in Milwaukee, and I had his wife—he had passed away—and he was a big influence on me, and I had her come in because I felt that was necessary. So it was really good—a tremendous feeling of accomplishment at that point.

The one thing that went through my mind was: we aren't going to win a game for like twenty. There are all of these emotions, and then you go you know what? We'll be fine. And then you start looking at some of your lineups, and you know they are good hockey players, but they aren't necessarily great hockey players. You just have to be a hardworking team who makes it hard to play games and not make any excuses for the way that we don't have this or that. One of the things we did was no excuses; let's not make excuses for who we are or how we're doing. It's all up to us. I think that year it was pretty successful. I think we won twenty-eight games, which is one of the better expansion teams at that point.

I remember the whole warm-up, everyone was standing, and the whole game everyone was standing. They didn't have the cadence of an NHL game down yet, but we lost that first game one to nothing I think.

The first game was a 1–0 loss to the Florida Panthers, but it didn't take long for the team to register its first victory, a 3–2 win over the Carolina Hurricanes on October 13, 1998.

"Yeah, everybody wants to win, and the fans don't know, in the untraditional market, if they have a good team or a bad team, they just have a team," said Trotz. "Everybody thinks that you have a good team, that you're an expansion team and you probably aren't going to be that great. But they came!"

The first season for the Nashville Predators saw them finish 28-47-7, placing them second to last in the Western Conference and third to last in the league. They finished ahead of the Islanders and Canucks in the league that season, certainly not abysmal for the first season as a team. The first few seasons are rough on an expansion team as it tries to establish itself. One thing stood out from the start, though, and that was the fan support behind the team.

"First, I came in with the idea that this was going to be brutal, like a Winnipeg, Washington or Long Island, where you are lucky to get twelve wins, and they come up with twenty-eight," said Pete Weber.

I think the first indication I got that this would be a great area was on opening night against Florida; there was a standing ovation for the opening faceoff. You just don't see that any place. We didn't score that night, and my worst memory of that first season was not being able to call the team's first goal—it didn't go in the net. We had to wait for video review, which ascertained the rules at that time, had the net not been knocked off its mooring, Andrew Burnett's shot would have gone in. So I was robbed of that opportunity to call the first goal. I felt a little cheated with that.

But the first year, the first ice storm right before Christmas, the game with Detroit, and people are calling the offices wondering if the game was going to be postponed, but we still saw fifteen thousand people for that game. I drove to meet the family in Knoxville for Christmas the next day, and once I got past Mt. Juliet, it was clear sailing. Talk about a localized ice storm! It reminds me of Buffalo if you haven't been there twenty years, and having seen games where three to five thousand people show up. And ironically enough, it was the Los Angeles Kings in town, and some of their reporters came not exactly dressed for the possibilities of that weather, so that was always fun. These people are a very hearty lot, probably more so than the football fans who[m] I have seen skip out on games in November and December.

The all-time best was the night where the Hurricanes were in town and a tornado was hitting downtown Nashville. People were being asked to go into the passageway between Bridgestone and the old convention center because that was the best place; they didn't want them around all of the

Predators fans cheering. *Don Olea Photography.*

glass we had on the concourse. Weather has played a large role. This year we had an ice storm, and I couldn't get out of my house—I live at the top of a hill—really until 4:00 p.m. on Tuesday, and I got here in time to do the game.

Welcome to the Cell Block

There are many arenas and stadiums throughout the world known for rabid fan bases or even sections of fans that tend to be the most rowdy. It's not any different for the Nashville Predators. What is different, however, is how section 303 became the Cell Block that everyone knows it is today. Obviously, every team has to start somewhere with fans turning into diehards, but a few people got together on opening night and just simply wanted to have fun. Mark Hollingsworth is known to many as "the warden" of the Cell Block. It was the background of minor-league hockey that he and his friends shared that helped turn the Cell Block into one of the most known sections in all of the NHL.

"My whole group of friends wanted to get tickets together," said Hollingsworth, recalling the moment when Nashville was awarded an NHL team.

A bit of backstory on that: I had a group of about six or eight friends that all went to the Nashville Knights games for years. We loved that fun, wild, minor-league experience. I had been a hockey fan for twenty-five years before that, and a lot of my other friends had not been. They were from different parts of the country that had not been exposed to hockey, but when they came to Knights games with me, they loved it. So then we had the idea of buying seats together for the Preds, even though we didn't know their name yet. When they finally had the day when you could go out and pick your season tickets where you wanted to sit, the reason that we chose 303 was because they were the cheapest seats, and also from my experience, when you're in a corner and elevated, that's where all the scouts sit and watch teams play and you can see the plays on the ice and feel the aura of the entire arena. We could see the benches from that angle and see the coaches going crazy and stuff like that. So we all got tickets there, and it wasn't strategic about the number 303. I had also been a writer for a publication called Hockey Inc., and I would interview teams from pros to juniors and how they marketed themselves. I would drive around the country a lot and see a lot of games, especially when minor-league hockey was in its heyday. In going around the country, and going to a lot of college games growing up, I would keep a list of all the fun chants and weird cheers that would go on. I had some favorite franchises like the Columbus Chill because they were very irreverent with the way they marketed the team. That's really what you need to do in a new hockey market is make people feel like they're a part of something—because, God knows, it's going to be years before they're a competitive team on the ice.

So we had fun at the minor-league games incorporating some of those things; now we have a major-league team, let's get serious about our fun. My buddies and I made a pact that we were going to be idiots together. We were going to do these chants whether anyone else did them or not. That first season, the Predators chose not to have any preseason games in Nashville. There was no way of meeting anyone in your section until opening night. Here we are, packed arena, everyone in anticipation, and about fifteen minutes before puck drop, I just stood up and I asked for everyone's attention and introduced myself and my friends as "a bunch of idiots that will have fun at every game no matter what the score." We were going to give the referees a horrible time and really taunt the other team. We knew that the Predators were not going to be very good, but we wanted to have fun. Most of the people around us seemed all right with it, so it started.

We were having fun with it, and some people asked us to print off some of the basic cheers because they didn't exactly know what was going on. So I made a sheet of stuff and would hand it out to people. We started to circulate, and by about the middle of the season, I started making signs and bringing them to help people get on board quicker with particular chants. It developed into this thing, and we just started calling ourselves the crazy idiots in section 303. Toward the end of the season, I got more formal printing up the sheets and would distribute them up and down every row. One of the guys said we should start a website, and we started to get a lot of hits.

By the second season, we were running. We had a lot of ideas between seasons. We had slap shot parties and get-togethers. There was a growing movement of people that thought the sport was exciting, and they loved coming to the games. And they especially loved 303. People were starting to transfer to 303 from other parts of the arena. By the third season, the Predators told us that 303 was, by far, the most requested section in the building, and nearly every seat was sold out as *a season ticket. It was the only section in the arena that was like that, and it spilled over into 302 and 304. We wanted games to be a fun thing to do and wanted Nashville Predators games to have some sort of unique quality that no other team had.*

So the section had established itself as the "super fans" for the Predators. All it really needed was an actual name, something it could be called that was more than just "section 303." With the close relationship between the fans and Nashville management, management got to work on helping to brand the section.

"It was during that second season [that] the head of game operations and I became good friends," said Hollingsworth.

We would get together regularly to tap into what the fans were thinking. Basically, they wanted to come up with a name for 303. The core group got together and shot ideas around, but we couldn't come up with anything. So then the Predators came to us and suggested Cell Block 303. I was sort of indifferent to it, but other people thought it worked because we were inmates and crazies that couldn't be confined. We had come up with the logo of the smiley face, but when they put the hat on it and put it behind bars, we thought it was pretty cool. They made the big banner, and we started to incorporate that stuff on our website. Over the years, we probably distributed over fifteen thousand chant sheets at the games.

Over the years, team performance in some games has been better than others, which is understandable. The fact still remains, though, that the Cell Block has created chants and cheers that still go strong to this day at Bridgestone Arena. While there will always be controversy over the saying "You suck!" it's still present close to twenty years later. It's made such an impact on how the arena is viewed by the league that mentions and images of the Cell Block, including its banner, have been made in the NHL franchise of video games by EA Sports.

"It's great that a lot of the chants were sort of engrained into the fabric of the Predators," said Hollingsworth. "The front office was very appreciative that we helped created that energy there. Would it have happened otherwise? I don't know, but there were chants that wouldn't have happened if not for us. Barry Trotz used to call us the igniter as the group that got things going. It was great to get recognition like that."

After the first season, the foundation had been laid. Professional hockey was now a part of Nashville. Exciting times were ahead for the city and the organization. Throughout its history, only one dark cloud hovered over the team, but the team and the fans would emerge from it stronger than ever before.

2
MAKING AN IMPACT ON PLAYERS

Since the start, Barry Trotz always spoke of "the Predator way." He was referring to blue collar–type players who outworked the opponent even though on paper their skills weren't necessarily evenly matched. Even under a new head coach, this mantra still rings true for the team: hardworking and outperforming. This can be seen in every Predators team. While it may not have been the most fruitful in terms of prospects in years it missed the playoffs, Nashville was never horrible enough to get the likes of Sidney Crosby and Jonathan Toews. The teams are always competitive. To some, it is frustrating. To others, it shows not just the work ethic of the team but also what's expected of the organization.

This all goes back to what Barry Trotz instilled in his players from the beginning. From original Predators to current ones, they all understand what it means to play Nashville Predators hockey. In his fifteen years at the helm, Barry Trotz was the right person for the job at the right time. Not only did he become the face of hockey in Nashville, but he also embraced that role.

Past players always speak not only of how much they love the city of Nashville but also how much of an impact Barry Trotz had on them and the team in general. When players and fans alike look back on the first fifteen years of the Nashville Predators, the only face that was on the bench for all of them belonged to Barry Trotz.

THE RAT: CLIFF RONNING

When NHL veteran Cliff Ronning was traded to the Nashville Predators just nine games into the inaugural season, he came to a team in need of veteran leadership. Trotz gave him that opportunity.

"When I first came here, we were in a little bit of shock, but I didn't know hardly a thing about Nashville," said Ronning. "I knew it was a town that had country music. I was very fortunate that the coaching staff and general manager were very welcoming to my family coming here, treating me like a veteran but also getting an opportunity to grow as a leader, as a hockey player, and I think I was put in that role to help the younger guys stay focused at the task at hand, and that is playing hockey to the best of your ability."

Ronning suited up for the Predators for four seasons. In those seasons, he played a vital role in mentoring younger players, as well as providing the team with much-needed offense.

"Being a smaller player, I never took a shift off," said Ronning. "That was just my makeup, that every shift I had to go hard because of my size. Maybe that transcended down to the other players—that one of your older players is one of the harder workers, much like Fisher, a guy that works every shift, and it sets the tone. Being in that situation taught me a lot as a person and how important it is to help give players confidence when they are down or give them good feedback to make them go even harder the next game."

It wasn't just the coach who helped mold the mindset of Predators hockey. Veterans like Ronning were the best examples of it with how they played. When asked if Barry Trotz was the right coach at the right time, Ronning said:

Absolutely. Barry Trotz is a guy who set the tone. He was a very honest coach, a players' coach, and he demanded guys to work hard and to work hard for one reason and that was the sweater that you had [with] *the Predators logo—you are playing for the team. Fitzgerald was the first captain, and he was a great captain because he wasn't the best player, but I can tell you he made sure that everyone in the dressing room was on the same page. Trotz was great at making everyone realize you go much further as a team than as an individual, and I think that is why he lasted so long there because he was doing such a great job, and it became time to move on for both parties and get a new type of coach in there to excite the team for years to come.*

When looking back on his time in Nashville, Ronning is reminded of how well the organization treated the players. He took to heart the opportunity he had as an older player to be a leader on an expansion team. Not only does he fondly recall his time on the ice, but he also remembers the generosity of the fans.

"When I look back, when I played my 1,000th game as an NHL player, David Poile had that one game for me when they dropped the puck and had a little ceremony," said Ronning. "But I think what I will always remember the most is the fans. The Predators fans are so warm, and they are different from other fans. They are very encouraging, and I think at all costs they want to win, but they also want to see a team that gives everything they have. For me, it was easy…to try my best whenever I got on the ice. It was a good fit."

Players come and go in hockey. It's a business. So many Predators alumni have made their way back, though. When they do, they see how much hockey has continued to grow in middle Tennessee. Ronning, who is the vice-president and co-founder of BASE Hockey, still makes frequent trips to the Nashville area.

"It's amazing to see the growth [of hockey]," said Ronning.

When we first started there, everyone remembers the headsets on explaining the game and different rules, but we never saw kids like up in Canada playing road hockey. We would love to see kids one day out on the streets playing hockey. That is something you see now—that excitement is there, and it has come from hard work from the organization doing grass-roots, getting out in the communities, and to me I think of all the teams in the NHL, they are one of the best at reaching out to their fans.

MITCH KORN AND TOMAS VOKOUN

Goaltending has always been a strong suit in Nashville. When one is down on his luck, another could easily step right in and do the job. It's almost been like clockwork for the Predators. Without the Predators, goaltender Tomas Vokoun would not have had the career he did. Picked up in the expansion draft, Vokoun was given a fresh start, a new opportunity to prove he belonged in the NHL.

"It is something you're looking for, especially being a player and in a situation where you feel like you're probably not going to be given a chance

Tomas Vokoun stops a Jonathan Cheechoo (Sharks) shot. *Don Olea Photography.*

for whatever reason that is. You look for a fresh start, and I think a fresh set of eyes looking for different people," said Vokoun. "I was fortunate enough to get that with the expansion draft and being able to come here. This franchise was forming and starting, and everybody started with a clean sheet; there were no set ways, no previous relationships. I think in my situation, it was the perfect environment for me to be in."

There are so many memories that fans carry with them about Vokoun. He recorded the first shutout for the team on January 15, 1999, a 2–0 victory over the Phoenix Coyotes in Nashville.

"It's one of those things when I get asked this question, there are a lot of downsides when playing for an expansion team as a goalie," said Vokoun.

> *There are things you can be proud of, and no matter how many games you win, there is always a chance someone will come after you, and you're going to play more games, win more games. But if you win the first game or get the first shutout, whatever you do first, it is impossible to break, so I am proud of every achievement. It wasn't handed to me. I had to work for it, so there is no reason not to feel good about something you did. Getting a shutout in the NHL is a big thing for a goalie. I was put in that situation to be able to be the first.*

Much of Vokoun's success can be attributed to former goaltending coach, Mitch Korn. Korn did wonders with the goalies in the Nashville system. He helped take goaltenders who at first didn't seem like they would be successful and turned them into winners.

"I think [Korn] made me understand it's not about today or tomorrow, it's about the long term," said Vokoun.

The position takes time to mature with the person. We go through growing pains, and it is important to learn from them and understand they are part of the process. Don't get derailed by setbacks; everyone will have them. He was a great mentor who had been through it before. He knew lots of stuff I was going through, not just hockey but personal life—like being from a different country and adjusting to life in a different country, people have expectations of you. I definitely owe him a lot for what I got from hockey, and he was a big part of the success I had, not just here but moving to different stops in my career.

Mitch Korn's impact was seen in a plethora of goalies who came through Nashville. Without his impact and the training he gave the goaltenders and other coaches, the Predators' success could easily be questioned.

"I worked at Miami University for thirty years. I started at Miami shortly after the program went varsity and the arena opened," said Korn.

My job there was literally to be a builder, to orchestrate most of the programs that began and started—the whole nine yards. That is what this was like. It was starting a franchise, starting from scratch, watching and watering the flowers and watching them grow. It was the same way at Miami. You look at them now, and they are one of the top five teams in the country, and this was no different. To watch Mike Dunham become a viable goalie, a great asset that turned into a great asset for David to train. The growth of Vokoun, even Chris Mason. Dan Ellis never played better than when he was here, and obviously the modern era of Pekka now. I am proud of all that. It was a great run and awesome to get to start from the ground up.

Korn and Trotz have basically been a package deal. They worked well together in Nashville, and Trotz is extremely thankful for what Korn was able to do with goalies for the Predators.

"I think you can probably put Mitch's contribution to goaltending in Nashville on the top of the list," said Trotz in regards to how important Korn was to the Predators.

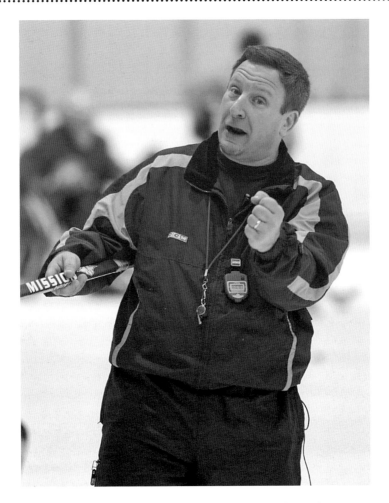

Mitch Korn, goaltending coach (1998–2014). *Don Olea Photography*.

You can't have any success if you don't have goaltending. Mitch really stabilized our goaltending, and one of the things we found out early was—and this was the greatest thing, I think—he has handled goaltenders in every which way, and he has handled great goaltenders and he has handled Hall of Fame goaltenders. The thing that was great about Mitch was, you look back at it now, is that we had two backup goaltenders who really won. Over a couple of years, he had to change Mike's [Dunham] mindset of fighting through stuff. Mike used to get worked up and now he is amped up every day, and he had to change a whole mindset.

Tomas Vokoun was discarded; they didn't have any need for him, and he came to our organization as probably the fourth or fifth goalie. And lo and behold, before the end of the season, he is our number one goalie and is taking over the job over Mike. When you have expansion players, one of the things that happens is those are the guys that are always on the fringe, so no one holds great self-confidence. So I learned this fairly early: you have to be really positive with these guys. Every time they didn't have a good game, Coach would be mad at them or they would get sent out to the minors. Mitch had to work with goaltenders that didn't have a lot of self-confidence because they were backups or minor-league guys. He worked diligently with them. They grew to believe and became fan favorites—Mike Dunham and Tomas Vokoun. Your goalies are going to be your favorite players because they are going to get a lot of work.

"You can't win without a goalie," said Terry Crisp.

I don't care where you are or whether it is the regular season or the playoffs, you don't win in this league. I still haven't ascertained yet who would be the scout that you would be like, oh, this guy can pick goaltenders. Now, obviously, when they picked them, Mitch Korn was a man who went to work and helped them along and made them a lot better in their chosen careers. Whoever did our scouting was over in Europe finding them and doing a hell of a job. We took Tomas Vokoun from Montreal, and he was done with them, and when we got Dan Ellis, Chris Mason, all the guys down the list. Every time I will say this—and I coached for twenty-plus years—it was amazing when I had a great goalie [say] what a great coach I was.

David Poile knows how important of a role Mitch Korn played for the Predators:

Part of my history, going back to the Washington Capitals, is that we had a really good team. Sometimes our goaltending wasn't enough to get us over the hump or win playoff rounds or compete for the Stanley Cup. I put that in my direction philosophy—to try as best as possible to have the best goaltending, and we have. Mitch Korn has done a fabulous job with mentoring them, and when you think back, they are on their seventeenth year, and we have two goalies in Rinne and Vokoun—and you can look this up to be more accurate—are probably over half of our wins, and we probably had five goaltenders that have 99 percent of our wins. It's great to have that consistency. Having four or five goalies over twenty years is pretty good.

Vokoun was another product of the Predator way. He earned every start he had. Being a part of an expansion team helped mold the team into a family, and that's something he'll never forget.

"This organization was always run with high expectations on and off the ice," said Vokoun.

From the moment the team started here, I think they understood they were going to have to grow their own fans. This wasn't a city where you come in and there is going to be a lineup, maybe the first season, but after that you lose that wow factor and the reality sets in. You don't have the star players, you don't have the fifty wins, you don't have a lot of things, and that persistence and being able to grow their own players and draft right and do it with a solid base…I think anything you do in life as a business or in sports or in your personal life, you need a good base, and I think these people came in and said let's build a base and we can always feel good about our core.

I think they always pick players not just on their skill or hockey abilities but also people they know who are good people and will fit here and help them make this environment a hockey town. In my opinion, they always kept that in mind. It wasn't always "let's find the best player we can and bring him here." There are variables to who you bring and draft. We always had a great locker room here, and obviously I have tremendous respect for Barry, not just from a professional point of view as a coach, but he's a very good person who cares about the people who work for him. Most of the time that's the case, but not always, and I think it is something you can take away from hockey, relationships like that. The day I retired, I got a phone call from him, and coincidentally they were in Florida, so I went to see him and Mitch…just stuff like that. We weren't just people who worked together for a few years, we are people who can get together and talk and treat each other as friends.

As a fan favorite then and now, Vokoun, like other alumni, shares a bond with the fans. There's a special connection that forms between fans and the players. There's a true appreciation on both sides.

"It feels good. I think everything you do in life, if it matters to you and you work hard, feels good to be recognized for all your hard work in every aspect," said Vokoun.

Tomas Vokoun. *Don Olea Photography.*

I got more welcome the first day I stepped on the ice here, and I always try to keep that in mind. I tried to be as involved with the fans and community as I could, and I understood there is a responsibility with that, too—you have to perform and make sure you know people sacrifice a lot of their lives to be fans and come to the games. It isn't the cheapest thing in the world, and they have to see that effort every single day, not nine times out of ten.

THE GOALTENDER WHO NEVER WAS: JAMIE ALLISON

Though many players from the pre–first playoff series days were around for only a few years, Nashville has remained with them.

"It was, I don't want to say a dream come true because that sounds kind of cliché, but I remember when they first came into the league," said Jamie Allison.

I always said because I was a singer first and foremost, I would love to play in Nashville, and it just worked out for me that I was able to sign there for one year, and I can't tell you how I excited I was to come. When I came, David Poile told me I was going to Milwaukee, that I was not going to be part of the Predators team that year, and I said, "With all due respect, David, I am going to make the team this year." And fortunately for me, I did!

Hard work helped Allison make the team in the 2003–04 season. That, coupled with an injury on the blue line, helped cement his spot.

"I think it was a bit of luck and determination," said Allison.

I didn't really change my game to be honest. I remember that year Jason York had suffered an injury to his eye, and it just so happen they needed a spot on defense. When I came in, I filled a specific role for them. I guess I added some toughness to the blue line that they needed, and just timing wise it worked out perfectly. I stayed a little bit longer than I thought, then next thing I know, I'm there for two years. And the best two years of my career.

As he mentioned, Allison loved to sing—so much so that he even performed at Petey's Preds Party, a benefit for the Brent Peterson for Parkinson's Foundation and the Nashville Predators Foundation. One of his favorite memories revolves around his vocal talents.

"I was a singer as well, and I got to do a lot of cool things there in Nashville outside of hockey," said Allison.

I remember the team—after one game, I was asked to do a show for charity. It was just me and my guitar, and the whole team showed up, and I got to do a little show for the boys. It was a fun experience for me. At the old Ryman Auditorium, I did a piece for TSN, which was really cool. We had an open mic contest with them where a bunch of guys in the league had a competition, and voters would call in and vote. Anyways, I got to do a lot of fun things outside of hockey, but the hockey was great, my favorite time as a hockey player.

A moment that will live in infamy for the Predators is also a moment that Barry Trotz calls one of his biggest regrets as a coach. On December 13, 2005, goaltender Chris Mason was injured during warm-ups against the Florida Panthers. Brian Finley was set to get the start, and Jamie Allison, who was to be scratched, would dress as the backup goaltender. As Allison recalls:

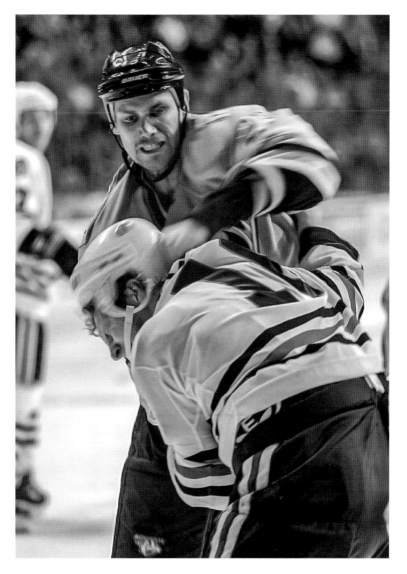

Jamie Allison was never afraid to drop the gloves. *Don Olea Photography.*

What happened was before the game, Tomas Vokoun was injured already, so we had Chris Mason as our starter. In warm-ups, Chris Mason got injured, pulled his groin or something, so we literally had our backup goalie, who has just been called up starting, and we didn't have a backup for him. So, being in the dressing room that night, I was told I wasn't going to play. I was a little frustrated, of course, so I am sitting there, and I see Trotz walk by and see his frustration because he doesn't have a backup goalie, and I jokingly throw out, "I'll suit up!" not thinking he would ever entertain that option. Next thing I know, he is coming out of his coach's office, and he says, "Alli, put on the equipment." And I just kind of look at him like really? And he said, "Yes, you're backing up."

I was obviously nervous, excited kind of, everything you can imagine. That had never happened before that I had ever heard of, so I put on Tomas Vokoun's equipment, which happened to fit perfectly, and I remember sitting on the bench and Kerry Frazier, the referee, came by and looks at me, does a double take and goes, "What are you doing in goalie equipment?" He had a good laugh. He happened to have a puck on him, and he threw it and said, "Heads up!" And of course I missed it, I even had the glove on, so he said, "They better not put you in!" So the game went on. Halfway through the second period, we were down; we were getting beaten pretty badly, and I kept looking at Trotz, winking at him like, "Are you going to put me in?" And he kept smiling at me, and he didn't. I really did want to go in—at least for a couple of shots—so it's too bad I didn't get to go in. But I remember Trotz just last year at Petey's Party said in his speech that his biggest regret in hockey, in all of his coaching, was that he didn't put me in that game. It was a really good experience and a good story. I am one of the only players who had played center, wing, defense and goalie in the NHL, so I guess I hold one record.

Unfortunately for Allison, he didn't get the call until right after warm-ups and couldn't even take a shot to get prepared.

"No, I didn't," said Allison on being able to take shots. "It happened after warm-ups. I literally put the equipment on, skated around for a minute to get used to the equipment and pace, but I am not very flexible, so if I ever did go in there, I would be the old-school guy, straight-legged guy."

Trotz looked back and thought he should have given Allison that one shot, even if just for a few shifts.

"Brian [Finley] had to be the goalie, who didn't have a particularly good night," said Trotz.

Two things went through my head. I was still young enough in the coaching fraternity that I thought it wouldn't look right if I put him in, he's not a goalie, I can't do it. As the years have passed and I have been in the game a lot longer, I wish I would have put him in because those are great stories and ones you remember. We were down six to three with ten minutes to go or something like that, and I probably should have just done it and made a good story out of it. Jamie came back for a function, and I told him if I could re-do anything, I wish I could have put him in.

For being with the team only two seasons, Jamie Allison not only has wonderful memories in Nashville but also makes sure to defend the city and its place in the hockey world.

"It's funny," said Allison.

I get frustrated up here in Canada hearing about these smaller market teams in the States, nontraditional hockey markets that struggle and we kind of bring down the league, and ever since I have been in Nashville, even playing against them, it always seems to me that the arena is full, the fans are passionate and as far as the players go, you come off the ice and out of the rink, you have your own life, you aren't bombarded every day.

As far as the hockey goes, it's an exciting place to play in! They love their hockey, and it seems to be getting better every year. I am really happy to see this year. I was sad to see Trotz go, but maybe it was time for a transition for everybody. Trotz is doing good this year, and I am glad to see that, it just seems that the city is getting better and better. They love the hockey, and it's never really a change. I can't say that it has grown to me, maybe outside of hockey, maybe some of the youth hockey hopefully is growing more and more, but it has always been a great hockey market.

Mark Jamie down as another successful Predators alumnus who has continued on with hockey after playing professionally. Allison recently opened the Oakville Hockey Academy in Oakville, Ontario, where he and his staff will help train future NHL stars.

BRIDGING THE GAP: SCOTT WALKER

Another continued fan favorite is Scott Walker. During the 1998 expansion draft, Walker was another player whom Nashville claimed. Like Vokoun, Walker is thankful for the opportunity given to him by the Predators.

"First of all, I loved coming here," said Walker.

They gave me a chance to be a full-time NHLer. I knew my role when I came down, and they helped me continue to develop as a hockey player.

Mostly, it's one of those things when you come in on an expansion year, nobody knew anyone. When you go to any other team, there are guys that have already been there, and they have connections in the town. For us, nobody had those little things going on, so we really were a tight team. We stuck together. When everybody is unfamiliar, the thing you're most familiar with is each other. I think for me, that was the most fun part.

We weren't a real great hockey team, but we worked hard. We worked hard in practice, worked hard in games. Barry did a great job instilling a system that I think we needed at that time. We tried to do everything he said. It was a lot of fun and very successful. I made great, lifelong friends that still live in Nashville that we visit and talk to. A lot of them were fans and neighbors. Players I still talk to are obviously Greg Johnson, Tom Fitzgerald, even Bill Houlder once in awhile. It was quite a group of guys.

That attitude of being a hardworking team is what gave fans such a connection to the early teams. For Walker, it was his hard-nosed, gritty style that made fans go wild. Walker could lay out a big hit, drop the gloves and score goals—easy markers for becoming a fan favorite. Throughout his seven

Scott Walker donning the infamous mustard yellow jersey. *Don Olea Photography*.

years with the Predators, Walker was able to witness how much hockey grew in the area. He witnessed it firsthand.

"The first year I was there, they had passionate fans, but they also had new fans to hockey," said Walker. "Some of the questions I got were just, to me, funny questions—just questions that you wouldn't hear anywhere else. Then, by the time I left, I had people critiquing my game, whether I was at the mall or a restaurant. That's when I knew it was catching on. When they start critiquing the power play or penalty kill and five-on-five, saying you guys should have done this or that, then I knew they get it."

It's a running theme that past players have wonderful things to say about the community and the organization. It's the culture that playing for the Predators instills that lives on with them.

"Even today, you have star players making lots of money and all those things, but I still think the work ethic and culture we set early on right from Tom Fitzgerald, our captain, from Barry to David Poile, right through the whole organization, and it comes from your top line players right down to your scratches," said Walker. "It set the franchise on the right footing with great culture and great work ethic and great people. It's amazing how far that can reach now, looking [back] twenty years later. I still think that people go there thinking it's a great place to play, work hard and embrace the community."

Walker was one of the few bridges between the expansion-era teams and the playoff-bound teams. He lived through the struggle of the early years but was also a part of the first two playoff teams for Nashville. His leadership and stability helped make him a staple for Predators fans, and he's still remembered well today.

A History of Caring

It would be an understatement to say that certain players made special connections with the fans. Some players just had a special bond with the fan base. More often than not, it was the players willing to drop their gloves on the ice. Many of the players—Jordin Tootoo, Wade Belak and Brian McGrattan included—all had a certain connection with fans. For Tootoo and McGrattan, the Nashville Predators proved to be a beacon of light. Both suffered from substance abuse at some point in their careers, and Nashville was there to help them either in recovery or in continued support. In the

3
A RIVALRY BEGINS

In the summer of 1990, the General Motors Corporation opened an automotive manufacturing facility to build Saturn vehicles in Spring Hill, Tennessee. With plants closing all around Detroit, Michigan, and its suburbs, the new plant brought an opportunity to those families with laid-off workers. With a steady influx of Michiganders heading to Tennessee, sports allegiances followed—most notably that of the Detroit Red Wings.

With Nashville being awarded an NHL franchise, excitement grew not only among locals ready to experience NHL hockey but also among those who left Michigan and would now have a chance to see their beloved Red Wings in action. This set up what would become a steady rivalry and a case of big brother versus little brother for years to come. The rivalry would also spurn a model of what the Nashville Predators aimed to become: perennial championship contenders. During this time, Nashville fans developed their own sense of celebration on the ice. It had been a long tradition for Red Wings fans to toss an octopus onto the ice. Predators fans took a page from this book and began tossing catfish onto the ice. Each time a catfish hit the ice, the arena would roar, and the tradition was set.

Following the 2014–15 season, the Nashville Predators held a 34-43-12 record against the Detroit Red Wings, according to the Nashville Predators website. While defeating the Red Wings in fives games during the 2012 Stanley Cup playoffs helped get them over the "little brother" hump, it was an uphill battle from the beginning.

Above: Celebration catfish on the ice. *Don Olea Photography*.

Left: Adam Hall. *Don Olea Photography*.

"We knew our talent pool wasn't even close to the Red Wings in the days I was playing against them wearing a Predators jersey," said former Predators forward Cliff Ronning.

> *They had the superstars and the high-flying wings, and we always felt in the dressing room if we can beat the best it is only going to make us better. That one game we played, our team had the game of our lives, and we actually beat them and outplayed them all over the ice. Right there, as a team, we realized anything can happen. Our roster definitely wasn't even close to theirs, but that night our team came together, and it was an amazing feeling, not just for the players but for the fans. It was a sense of pride.*

There are many games against the Red Wings that stand out in the minds of fans, starting with an 8–0 win on February 28, 2009, the first home playoff win and even what has been dubbed "fight night."

On October 30, 2003, during their first meeting of the season, the Nashville Predators and Detroit Red Wings combined for a total of 210 penalty minutes in Nashville's 5–3 victory. For the Predators, Jeremy Stevenson, Adam Hall, Scott Walker and Jamie Allison all dropped their gloves in what turned into a bloody battle on the ice.

"We were pretty good rivals, us and the Red Wings," said former Predators winger Jeremy Stevenson. "I tried to get the guys going, and [Darren] McCarty was in there. And one thing led to another during the game, and there were several fights. Then I fought another d-man at the end of the game. I think it's just who wants to be the bigger dog, and that's what started it. It was great [to get the win]. It showed the character of our team that year. We went out and did what we had to do to win."

Former Predators defenseman Jamie Allison remembers vividly his fight against Darren McCarty: "One of my fights with Darren McCarty was one of my favorite fights I ever got in—not that fighting is all I ever did. I consider myself a decent defenseman, but that was fun."

Playoff Rivals

It took a few years of building a team, but on April 11, 2004, the Nashville Predators hosted their first-ever playoff game: game three of the Western Conference Quarterfinal against the Detroit Red Wings. During regular season games, from the inception of the franchise throughout most of the first half of the team's existence, much of the arena would be filled with Red Wings red thanks to the exorbitant amount of northerners now living in the Nashville area. It was only fitting that the first playoff series be against Nashville's first and longest-standing rival.

For the team, getting into the playoffs that year wasn't an easy feat. The Predators had to battle until the very end of the season just to sneak in. While Nashville lost the series 4-2, it generated plenty of momentum for the fans and gave them a true taste of what was yet to come.

Barry Trotz detailed the eventual 4-2 series loss:

> *It was huge. It was a struggle just to get in. We got in the playoffs in just the last couple of games in the season, fighting tooth and nail to get in. We go into Detroit, and I think they had a real top in team, the payroll was close to $72 million back then, and we were probably about $15 million back then. It was very David and Goliath. We had a lot of respect for Detroit because of what they had done and who was coaching them and a number of Hall of Fame players they had, but at the same time we said, you know, we are going to play these guys hard, and they will remember playing us. I remember we changed a lot of their system just to give them a different look and trying to come up with an angle to get a win, and we ended up scoring in the first playoff game on the first shift—Adam Hall from Scott Hartnell I believe—and it gave us a little belief when we scored right away. We lost the first two games in Detroit, and one of the things we talked about when we were flying back to Nashville, we had kind of a funny schedule, and I do remember, I said, they beat us the first two games and the Red Wings landed just ahead of us, and I said to the bus driver I will give you a hundred bucks if you pass their bus and get to the hotel before them.*
>
> *We ended up winning the next two games, and I remember the first game we won back in our building. We were so loud that you had the white noise in your ear, and we won that game. One of the big producers covering that series said to me that game one they had trouble with their cameras, and I said why, and he said he called his guys and asked them to keep the cameras straight because the building was shaking it was so loud. It was a really special time because you really were David versus the Goliath, and back then our building would be filled with Red Wings fans, and it was one of the first times where it started to pull some of those Red Wings fans over to our side who lived in Nashville and ended up being the "Pred Wings." We lost in six games, but it was testament to the group that we were serious*

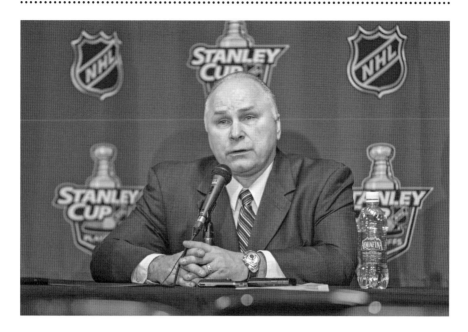

Barry Trotz addresses the media during the playoffs. *Don Olea Photography.*

underdogs who didn't play like it. Usually the teams we played in the playoffs went on to win cups.

General manager David Poile thought the series highlighted a big accomplishment for the club:

That sort of was the philosophy and the game plan, expansion era for an "x" number of years, hopefully shorter than longer, and once we get to be competitive, we want to stay competitive as long as we possibly could. I think, to a man, whether it be our scouts or management or hockey ops team or players, I think we realized we joined that competitive era. We tied the Red Wings 2–2 in the first four games, and I know talking to Kenny Holland that they were a bit nervous about us, but they won out. Probably just a bit of inexperience, but it was a great platform to the next year and to the increased belief that we were a competitive team.

Craig Leipold could barely contain his excitement. A team that he helped build from scratch had finally made it to the dance. His Predators were now one of sixteen teams that would compete for the Stanley Cup.

"It was one of the highs of my life," said Leipold.

I will never forget the day that we were on a road trip the last game of the year in Colorado. Edmonton had lost their game, and so as a result we made the playoffs that night. The next night, we played Colorado and [if we hadn't] beaten them—which we did—we would have made the playoffs anyway. The first "making the playoffs" is every team's goal. I felt like we had won the Stanley Cup. We came back from that road trip, and there were hundreds of people waiting for us at the airport when we landed just because we made the playoffs.

To go into a series against the iconic Detroit Red Wings with all of their superstars and to win two games at home, we really felt like we have made it, we are successful, we crossed that first very important bar that you set in life, and it was a couple of weeks I will never forget. I keep in touch with a lot of those guys until this day.

Former players have vivid memories of the first playoff series. For all of them, it was not only a relief but also something they realize was a reward for all of their hard work through the expansion years. Jeremy Stevenson, a player known more for his role as a fighter, has fond memories of what the team went through just to get to that point of the playoffs.

"It was awesome," he said.

I still remember flying in, and we were leaving Colorado watching a game. I think it was Edmonton and Vancouver, and Edmonton had to lose for us to get in, and they did. Then we had a big team meeting, the owner was there; it was just a great feeling to see this first step in the organization and to be a part of it. Seeing where they're at right now is such a big improvement, and I feel like the first time being in the playoffs meant something to me, it feels like I'm part of a tradition.

I remember coming to the game. It was a nice day, and I had a hard time getting into the rink because there were so many people downtown, and driving downtown they are all stopping you cheering and screaming, and that electricity downtown was awesome. We came in and blew out a big win, and it meant a lot to beat Detroit that first game. And the second game we won as well. I believe we had a lot of similar players; our team just gelled, and once you do that you can accomplish a lot. And that year we fought and scratched our way through everything, all the adversities, and we started a new tradition with the Nashville Predators and got to the playoffs.

Goaltender Tomas Vokoun knew that he was part of something special in helping lead the team to the playoffs. Vokoun started seventy-three games in the 2003–04 season, going 34-29-10.

"It was great," said Vokoun on being a part of that team.

> *It was a huge step for me personally that year. It was a huge step for this franchise, after all those years playing the last thirty games, knowing you aren't going to make it, coming in with high expectations every year and then being disappointed. We turned a corner and changed the perception people have about this team, and I am proud of it.*
>
> *I think there are a lot of teams who weren't able to do it in a modern-era expansion, some of them who are no longer in those cities, so it was a big moment for the team and for hockey. Even for hockey being in Nashville today, seeing how far it came along and what a hockey town it is now and the excitement the city has for their team and how the rink is run. It's a great fan experience for them to come to this rink.*

Not only do the players, coaches and executives remember everything from that season, but also Pete Weber can recall the buzz around the city. Making the playoffs for the first time generated a new kind of feeling around the city of Nashville. The Predators winning two games against the Red Wings also caused panic in Hockeytown, as no one expected an expansion team from the South to even put up a fight.

"It was fantastic," said Weber.

> *Everybody wondered, well you're in the Bible belt, and your first home playoff game is Easter Sunday afternoon? You're not going to have anybody in there! Wrong. It was an incredibly electric atmosphere. Tomas Vokoun had them flustered. In the two home games, he gave up one goal, one in the opener and a shutout in the second game. You lose the first two very tight games and win the two here, then we get back to Detroit, and we are staying out at the Ritz Carlton out in Dearborn, and then I pick up the newspaper from the newsstand downstairs and the* Detroit Free Press *had this headline: "Panic in Hockeytown." These are the guys who have been there and know how to get the job done; the headline writer thought there was panic, and that is one thing I won't forget.*

The Lockout

All of the buildup of success that the Nashville Predators experienced during the 2003–04 season was abruptly put on hold for the 2004–05 season—because it didn't happen. On September 16, 2004, the National Hockey League went on a shutdown that would kill the entire season, making it the first time in over eighty years that the Stanley Cup would not be awarded.

"I guess you'd have to say it's equal for everybody. This happened twice, and it's very disruptive and it can affect you, but for us it didn't too much," said David Poile on the lockout.

And he was right. The following season, the Nashville Predators made the playoffs again. This time, they actually acquired their biggest free agent signing for the team to date.

"The most interesting thing, I was back in western New York when the lockout ended, and then all of a sudden my phone is blowing up because Paul Kariya decided he wanted to come to Nashville," said Pete Weber.

Alexander Radulov. *Don Olea Photography*.

And I was interviewing Francisco Liriano at the ballpark in Rochester before he pitched that night and before he spoke much English, and I, at a baseball game, did more hockey interviews with the Canadian stations than I had done ever, and I mean ever. Even after the little problem in Scottsdale with Andrei Kostitsyn and Alex Radulov, more than at any other time.

So I think in a way that was the biggest jump-start for the return, and then obviously the two best seasons followed that: 106 and 110 points! Unfortunately, as you see, you get the wrong matchup, you get San Jose both times, and so those were very short lived, but that was a huge help. Then after the '07, that was when the sale of the franchise was announced, you want to talk about heart stopping. That was heart stopping!

As you can see, even with a lost season, it didn't change much in the Predators' plans. They had gone head-to-head with their perennial rival and even put a little bit of a scare in the Red Wings. The two teams would meet again in the 2008 Stanley Cup playoffs, where the Red Wings again defeated the Predators in six games.

It wasn't until the 2011–12 season that Nashville would finally get over the hump of defeating its rival in the playoffs, taking down Detroit in just five games in the Western Conference Quarterfinal. The series would be the last time the two foes would meet in the playoffs as divisional rivals, with realignment taking place after the 2012–13 lockout-shortened NHL season.

4

NO LONGER AN EXPANSION TEAM

While some would argue that the expansion era may have lasted longer, most will agree that with the Predators making their first playoff appearance, the expansion era was officially over. It was in the years following that the future of the Nashville Predators began to flourish.

Defenseman Dan Hamhuis became one of the first of a string of homegrown defensemen to take to the blue line for Nashville. Hamhuis was taken twelfth overall in 2001 and made his debut with the team in 2003.

"My early career through junior and those first few years, growing up in the town I did, I didn't know anything about the Western Hockey League I came through until I was in it," said Hamhuis.

> *I never imagined I would play in the NHL until I was in it, so it was kind of dream but not a realistic dream to me. To get drafted was surreal. I was really excited to be drafted by the Predators because I didn't think it would be as overwhelming as going to a big city like New York or Vancouver or Los Angeles. Looking back, it is certainly a great place for a young player to start a career and continue on with the type of people who live in this city and the type of people in this organization.*

Against the St. Louis Blues on October 16, 2003, Hamhuis potted his first career NHL goal. He still remembers exactly how it happened:

Dan Hamhuis handles the puck against the Carolina Hurricanes. *Don Olea Photography*.

I remember circling around the right side and getting the puck and dragging it across the top of the circles and taking a slap shot. It was Chris Osgood in the net, and I went to the glove side on him. I was really excited and surprised it had happened since it was only a week into the season. It was a relief to get that one out of the way.

The next season was cut due to a lockout. All of the momentum of the previous season was put on hold, but luckily for Hamhuis, he was able to play with American Hockey League affiliate the Milwaukee Admirals.

"I don't think it affected too much," said Hamhuis of the lockout affecting his development.

I think it helped a lot of the younger players on the team who went down to the AHL that year. We all had big roles on the team, which developed us as pros, and if you look at the years following the lockout, we had some really successful seasons. We brought in some free agents to complement the young depth that we have got.

Hamhuis was the first of a crop of blue liners that would make a big impact on the club. It was the systems that Nashville ran that helped him and others become successful.

"They were patient," said Hamhuis on the Predators.

> *I played two years in the minors in Milwaukee. We had good coaches here who did so much teaching. We spent so much time watching videos that I think some guys got annoyed from us watching so much, but in the end it taught us about the game, and we were held accountable for every mistake. We got a lot of opportunity here, too; they always played their young guys a lot of minutes, and that is what you need to develop.*

Even with new blood taking over the team, it was always a tightknit group, especially the first squad to head to the playoffs. It's one of Hamhuis's favorite memories

"That first year we made the playoffs was really exciting for the organization. It was the sixth season for the Predators, and it was a huge deal to make it," said Hamhuis. "We had a celebration that night, that's one thing. But overall, just the community and family environment that was established here from management and coaches and players. We always had such a tightknit group, and we were really embraced by the community. I loved being out and spending time in Nashville."

As it goes with being a business, when Hamhuis became a free agent in the summer of 2010, he left the organization to sign with the Vancouver Canucks, a team closer to his home in British Columbia. Following Hamhuis's drafting, however, came defensemen who would become the faces of the franchise for years to come.

THE ALL-AMERICAN DEFENSEMAN: RYAN SUTER

The 2003 NHL Entry Draft is widely considered a generational draft in regards to the talent that has seen success from that draft class. Three of the players that Nashville drafted in 2003 would go on to play a big role for the organization: Ryan Suter, Kevin Klein and Shea Weber. Out of the three, Weber, the current captain, was selected behind Suter and Klein, forty-ninth overall. Not only was it a phenomenal draft class for Nashville, but also the 2003 NHL Entry Draft took place in Nashville.

Ryan Suter. *Don Olea Photography*.

"It was neat. I think there were four or five of us defensemen," said Ryan Suter. "It was a good group of guys, and it was a lot of fun being drafted. The draft was here in Nashville, so we were all here earlier and got to hang out a couple of days before. It was great. The atmosphere here has always been awesome."

Suter was very complimentary of the core of young players that Paul Fenton helped bring through the system. Currently the assistant general manager, in Suter's development days, Fenton was the director of player personnel.

"I think Paul Fenton was the main guy when it came to all of us," said Suter. "He drafted Hamhuis, Hartnell, Upshall—some pretty good players. Paul was a big part of that. Nashville always stuck with their younger core guys and always gave them a chance, and I was very fortunate to be one of those guys."

Suter was also part of the first team to win a playoff series for the Predators. For five different playoff runs, Suter was on the blue line, including both times the team went on to the second round. First, it was against the Anaheim Ducks in six games in 2010–11 and then the Detroit Red Wings in five games in 2011–12.

"We felt like we could never win a series, and we won one finally," said Suter on winning the first series. "It was a fun team to be with, and they have always had a great coaching staff, and all of the older guys that have moved on to other teams. It has always been classy people that have been part of the organization."

When Suter became a free agent in the summer of 2012, he caught the ire of many Predators fans for signing a contract with the Minnesota Wild. In his time, Suter saw tremendous growth in youth hockey. It's something that he's been a part of wherever he has gone.

"When I first came here, there wasn't much youth hockey to speak of in the Nashville area," said Suter. "I know now they have three rinks here, so it's nice to see. The passion is here, the youth hockey is growing and they have done a really great job. I know when I was here, we had talked with the management and owners about trying to help develop that."

It's upsetting to fans when beloved players leave for other teams, but that's just the nature of the business. Following Suter's departure, another homegrown defender, Kevin Klein, was traded to the New York Rangers. The only remaining defenseman from that draft class (which also included Alexander Sulzer) is captain Shea Weber.

A MODEL FRANCHISE

As the team began to find its identity in the post-expansion era, general manager David Poile knew how he had to mold the team. The model team was a very successful division rival.

"We soon realized the model franchise for us was the Detroit Red Wings," said Poile.

They were winning Stanley Cups, they were successful every year and they played in our division, so we played them six times a year. Quickly, I think we realized we needed to have as many skilled players as possible to compete with them, so that was always a target, always a comparison, and the method of doing that was primarily through the draft. Again, trading off any assets we had to get younger players or to get draft picks, then putting ultimate faith in our amateur scouts, we could build a team through the draft.

The 2003 draft is what helped put the Predators on the map. Poile obviously knew that the players were skilled, but he did not go into the draft thinking he would get that much talent in one draft class. Did he know then how those three players would develop?

"Yes and no," said Poile. "The reason I say that is, philosophy and direction [are] really important, and we really felt that was a shortcoming of our team in the present and in the future, and we really put our mind to drafting defensemen in that draft. If you're pessimistic, you'd say you risked quality to get quantity, but as it turned out, it was quantity to get quality. That draft set us up for years."

It certainly set the team up for more years of success. While not selected in the first round, it can easily be said that Shea Weber has been the biggest pick taken from the 2003 draft.

Shea Weber taking the puck at the blue line against the Flames. *Don Olea Photography.*

"Once again, there is always a little bit of a story, whether it was good scouting—which it was—or a little bit of luck, we had drafted in the previous year in the second round a player by the name of Tomas Slovak, who you won't remember because he never turned out. But because he was our draft, I think we went to Kelowna a lot more than other teams, and I think we were very worried," said Poile.

> *The scouting process zoned in on their defense, and there was Shea Weber, who didn't get as much ice time. And for all of our guys going so often, his name kept coming up, and with a little bit of digging and information and going back, as big as he is today, he wasn't the biggest guy at that time, so he had a real good growth spurt. It was the right place at the right time. It was good scouting, and there was a reason for it, which was a negative as we found out, and it worked out really good for us.*

Shea Weber has been an important figure to the Nashville Predators. When Jason Arnott was traded to the New Jersey Devils, Shea Weber became the fifth captain in franchise history on July 8, 2010. So far, Weber is a four-time All Star and has been named an NHL First Team All Star and Second Team All Star twice each. Weber also brought home a gold medal with Canada in 2010 and 2014.

BLOCKBUSTER TRADES

Prior to the playoff run of 2007, the Predators made a blockbuster trade to acquire Hall of Famer Peter Forsberg from the Philadelphia Flyers. It was one of the biggest trades in Predators history to that point because of the accolades that Forsberg brought with him. Forsberg came to Nashville as a two-time Stanley Cup champion and both a Hart Memorial and Art Ross Trophy to his name, as well as two Olympic gold medals.

"We were in St. Louis, at Mike Shannon's restaurant, when my phone began to blow up about it," said Pete Weber.

> *Well, John Boruk, former Channel 2 reporter now working at Comcast SportsNet in Philadelphia, called me and said, "I think you got him! He's scratched from the lineup tonight." So I started making some calls. Yes we do have him coming here to Nashville, so that was a fun night, all the*

Above: Newly acquired Peter Forsberg puts on the Predators sweater. *Don Olea Photography*.

Left: Paul Kariya (left) and Steve Sullivan (right) celebrate a Predators goal. *Don Olea Photography*.

excitement. The closest to that would have been the first playoff year when we were in Columbus after a rare loss there. Barry Trotz told the guys Steve Sullivan was coming from Chicago, and to see that excitement surge you would have thought on that flight back to Nashville that the Predators had just won that game! But no, they effectively won a trade and brought a guy in, and it was a huge spark plug for the team.

Speaking of Sullivan, that trade will rank high in Predators history. Sullivan was not only the first postseason award winner for Nashville, but he also made quite the statement in his first game for the Predators after being acquired from the Chicago Blackhawks.

"Three shots, three goals, on the power play, essentially the same play each time, him and Kariya down low from one low circle to the other, and the quick one-timer—to see that, it was perfection to get started," said Weber. "You're supposed to get better, and effectively he did, but I can't think of a better debut that anyone has ever had for this team, not at all. Even Paul Kariya's first night, when we won the shootout against Anaheim, that was close to it."

AN OPPORTUNITY FOR A CAREER

As players come and go, the running theme is that Nashville has given them a chance. From Tomas Vokoun to Scott Walker, many teams had either given up or were done with them when the Predators gave them an opportunity to succeed.

"I loved it," said goaltender Anders Lindback on playing in Nashville. "It was my first NHL experience overall. I came into a great organization and a great group of guys. I think I developed a lot, and I had two really fun years. We made it to the second round of the playoffs for the first time in history, and that is a big thing. I really appreciated the whole defense. They really were amazing."

Forward Vern Fiddler says Nashville will always be special to him because it's where his career began.

"It's very special to come back here; it's where I started my career," said Fiddler. "My first son was born here, and we are always going to have a connection through that. It's just such a great city, and I don't think I could have asked for a better city to start my career. David Poile and Barry Trotz

Goaltender Anders Lindback. *Don Olea Photography.*

gave me every opportunity, not based on my pedigree but based on my work ethic, to have every chance I could to make this team, and it was a lot of fun while I played here."

Playing under Barry Trotz and in the Predators organization is what helped mold Fiddler into the player he is today. While he's no longer with the organization, it's thanks to the Predators that he had an opportunity to be an NHL player.

"I've always worked hard, but I definitely started to channel it in areas where Barry Trotz and Brent Peterson molded me to be the player I am," said Fiddler. "In the minors, I used to think of it a bit differently, and when I came here, they always made me focus on the things that I had to do to be in the NHL, which is killing penalties and being an energy guy."

Current Predator Eric Nystrom is a former teammate of Fiddler's from their days playing together with the Dallas Stars. He's one of the people who keeps the Nashville connection alive.

"I played with him a couple of years. We played on the same line so we are really close," said Fiddler. "Shea Weber and I both live in Kelowna in the

Vern Fiddler jaws with Phillippe Boucher of the Dallas Stars. *Don Olea Photography.*

off season, so I keep in touch with him. They've had a lot of face changes in there, but hopefully they can still have success."

Another player for whom Nashville played a major role in his start was Joel Ward. Prior to signing with the Predators in 2008, Ward had spent more of his time in the minor leagues. With Nashville, however, he made the opening night roster right out of camp. It didn't take long for Ward to tally his first career NHL goal either, which happened on October 10, 2008, against the St. Louis Blues.

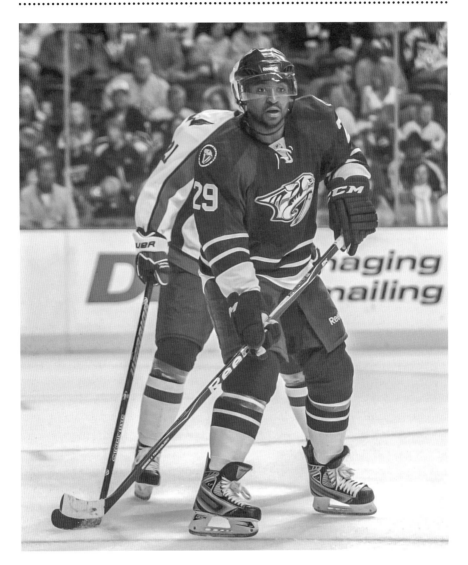

Joel Ward in a blue alternate jersey on the ice against the Washington Capitals. *Don Olea Photography.*

"I got a chance to play here and have an unbelievable moment. I can't say enough about it here. It was a great spot, and I was fortunate to be here," said Ward. "I always had a lot of fun. It was where I got my career going, so I am thankful to the organization for that. Barry gave me the opportunity to play and be a good professional and do the right things every day."

Ward was also a part of the first Predators team to see the second round of the playoffs.

"It was a great experience. Anytime you play in any playoffs it's fun, and to beat Anaheim and move forward," said Ward. "The building was electric, and the fan base here is unbelievable. It has always been loud, and I think we have won a lot of our games because of the fans here, and they have always been helpful, and I will always remember that about that series."

Since day one, the fan base has been what stands out to the players. Joel Ward is not an exception.

"Playing my first game to winning that series against Anaheim," said Ward on his favorite memories. "I have the memory of the fan base from coming in on a Saturday night game, there was always a fun time with the fans looking for a big win. The people, the city, they all embraced us really well, and it was a lot of fun."

If ever there were a hiccup in the history of the Predators, it would be following the 2006–07 season, when a change in ownership came. Original owner Craig Leipold was seeking to sell the franchise. Rumors soared about the team potentially being moved to Hamilton, Ontario, and even Kansas City.

Two months later, in July, fans and business owners held a rally in support of the team staying in Nashville. With local ownership stepping forward, the purchase was made official by the NHL in November 2007.

"I will never forget the rally that was here in July of that year, and Governor Bredesen and his wife had the sign 'Get your hands off our damn team' that was prominently displayed across both countries," said Pete Weber. "Thinking about that, that was huge to be able to do that. You know what was really miraculous was how quickly David Freeman got these disparate sources to come in and purchase a part of the team—that was mind-boggling to me. You don't just find deals that come together when you need that many different parts to it because usually you can find at least two or three people, but evidently I know that did not happen."

While at the time it seemed like a time of despair for Predators fans, the new era of local ownership almost seemed to bring with it a paradigm shift. In just a few years, the club would go on to experience its most successful seasons. It also brought with it a complete change of branding as the golden era began.

Following the offseason "fire sale," as it has been dubbed, the Predators front office had to do much retooling of the roster. Gone were the likes of

Predators fans at the rally for the team. *Don Olea Photography*.

Pete Weber and then Tennessee governor Phil Bredesen. *Don Olea Photography*.

Jeremy K. Gover holding a sign at the rally to keep the team. *Don Olea Photography*.

Tomas Vokoun, Scott Hartnell and Kimmo Timonen. New players were growing up in the system to take their place, and the team, surprisingly, once again made the playoffs. Credit for the success of that season following so much turmoil can easily go to Barry Trotz, who has always been known for getting the most out of his players, no matter the talent level of the team.

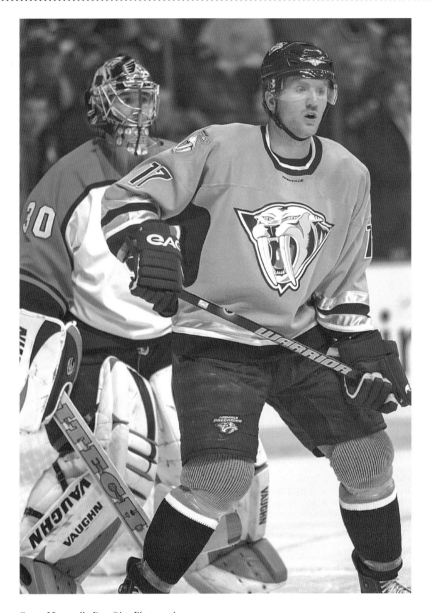

Scott Hartnell. *Don Olea Photography*.

The team would once again meet the Detroit Red Wings in the first round, where they would lose 4–2. As was a theme with multiple first-round opponents for the Predators, the Red Wings went on to win the Stanley Cup that season.

Patric Hornqvist parked in his usual residence: in front of a goalie. *Don Olea Photography.*

Following another early playoff exit, the Predators faced a tough season that saw them miss the playoffs for the first time in five seasons. After the disappointment of missing the playoffs, roster changes were inevitable the next season. For the 2009–10 season, more homegrown players with skill began to make an impact on the team. Colin Wilson made his debut, and Patric Hornqvist became a breakout player. Pekka Rinne solidified the crease, and the Predators were looking like a playoff team.

"We often tell the story, Barry and I. At development camp we had four goalies to look at, all drafts," said Mitch Korn. "There was another Finnish guy, a Russian guy, a Czech guy and then there was Pekka. I put him through a whole bunch of drills, and then they are going off the ice and Barry and I both looked at each other and said, 'That one!' And that one was Pekka."

Entering the playoffs in 2010, Nashville would face the Chicago Blackhawks for the first time in the postseason. It was a different Blackhawks team that now featured Jonathan Toews and Patrick Kane. On the bright side, the Predators won their first-ever away playoff game, but on the dark

Pekka Rinne. *Don Olea Photography*.

side, game five will forever live in infamy for not only the fans but also the players of that season's team.

With a 4–3 lead in game five and the series tied at two apiece, Nashville was given a power play with just over one minute in regulation. Begrudgingly to the team, Patrick Kane scored shorthanded to force the game into overtime. Just over a minute into overtime, Marian Hossa exited the penalty box and scored the game winner. Nashville would lose game six at home to the eventual Stanley Cup champions.

The next season, however, would bring fulfillment to not only the team but also a fan base that had been yearning for victory in the playoffs for over ten years.

5

THE GOLDEN AGE

In the summer of 2010, the front office of the Nashville Predators made two moves that would help put it at the forefront of being a successful franchise. The hiring of Jeff Cogen and Sean Henry helped the executive leadership of the organization gain tremendous experience. Cogen, who was part of the 1999 championship Dallas Stars team, was brought in to serve as the chief executive officer of the Nashville Predators. Henry, who was with the Tampa Bay Lightning during its Stanley Cup victory in 2004, was hired to serve as president and chief operating officer. Both men had the experience of not only winning but also growing the game of hockey in their respective markets.

"I think they know how to thump the tubs, to get that excitement going, and that is critical," said Pete Weber.

> *I remember interviewing Jeff the first day he came in, and maybe I hit him with something he was a little surprised about, but I knew what he had accomplished in Dallas with the Dr. Pepper sponsorship and opening up all these Dr. Pepper Star hockey centers and what that's done for hockey at the Metroplex in Dallas. I asked him if he was planning on doing the same thing here. Well, we've seen one open already and [are] likely to see some more and [are] looking forward to that. Once you can get the kids on the ice, sorry parents, you're hooked!*

Cogen and Henry have both been pivotal in growing the sport in the community by adding more rinks with the opening of Ford Ice Center in the fall of 2014. Not only that, but they've also played a pivotal role in increasing ticket sales and branding the team.

Henry came to Nashville wanting to gain new experiences after already achieving so much in his career. After being a part of multiple sports organizations, it was, overall, the message of chairman of the Nashville Predators Tom Cigarran that let him know this was where he belonged. The mindset of building a championship team inside a busy arena had been building in Henry for quite some time.

"When I started my career, I moved to Detroit, transferred there with my company, and the Pistons just won their second championship," said Henry.

There were a lot of guys there that turned it around. It was really neat to see this group that had a vision set a goal, and the goal was very simple: We're going to build a new arena, redefine the industry and be better than anyone's ever been. But most importantly, we're going to build this around a championship team. I was so envious in a very greedy way when I saw the bond and sense of accomplishment that they had. All through my career—and I was fortunate enough to be a part of a few organizations in doing some new things—it wasn't until I got to Tampa, when the Pistons bought them back then, we were probably the worst team in sports. Third ownership group in three years, the fan base was tortured through weird changes and I remember thinking, "Wow, I'm going to have an opportunity to do what those guys did just twenty to thirty years earlier." I remember I was talking to one of the guys who left the organization after that and was with another basketball team at the time. He was one of my early mentors. He said, "My whole career, I've sought to replicate what we had in Detroit, and I'll never find anything that special again." And I remember that it hit home with me, and that's what happened in Tampa. It was magical.

We took one of the worst-run buildings, a team that was struggling on every front, and built a real bond between hockey and business in the arena, melded it into one and united it with the community. What did we do? We ended up being one of the busiest buildings in the country for ten years straight; led the league in attendance one year; we had a couple seasons of straight sellouts; won a cup, obviously; and built around some young guys growing into superstars before our own eyes in front of a guy wearing number 35 [Nikolai Khabibulin] in net that dominated. It was so special, and you didn't even realize it until we sold the team, and we realized that the experience was that neat. The president of the team, one of my early mentors, was with the early Pistons group and then there, and I thought how lucky to have done this twice.

Then, Mr. Cigarran called, and they were looking to re-do how they ran this organization. We had some very keen visions on wanting to turn it over to businesspeople to run it. He wanted those people to form a natural bond with hockey in the community and change how the building was run. And I sat there listening to him, and I gave that speech a thousand times, and that's saying too much. But the funny thing was that my wall in Tampa was our goal, and it was in the shape of the Stanley Cup where we spelled out our goal. It didn't say "One Goal" on it, but it basically said: be the number-one venue in America built around a Stanley Cup championship team. I never said that to Tom during the interview process. I asked him what he wanted to achieve with this new way of setting the team up, and I'm a big believer in hiring the right people to run the team. Owner should own, manager manage, coaches coach, players play. And he said, "It's very simple. I like aggressive goals because why would you set any other goal?" And it gave me chills because it's something I've always said. He said word for word what's on the One Goal sheet, which is: be the best facility in America built around a Stanley Cup championship team. I honestly got goose bumps. I didn't care what the job, title or pay was; in that moment, I wanted to come work with Tom Cigarran. Combine that with the fact that you have the best general manager in the NHL who—you look at David's track record and all those years of drafting, growing, cultivating all-stars and then unfortunately not hav[ing] the resources to secure them. And you know what David can do. He's the best GM in the NHL, and I can't wait for us to win a cup to really celebrate that.

So they had that going for them, and I remember that I had seen eight or ten games here and a handful over at Adelphia Coliseum at the time, and every time I came here, whether there were nine thousand or fourteen thousand people in the building, the crowd and fans and the love they have for the team—we can do something really special here. More importantly, to quote my friend Harry Hutt, "I can catch magic here." I can be a part of something really special. Obviously, Jeff and I didn't know each other that well before coming here. We spent some time together when we both accepted the job. I realized that we're so much alike and so different in certain areas that it really will allow us to do some cool things. A lot of times when people come in in that new position, they blow out half the staff, bring in new people, and I never understood that. We had a shared vision—be the best team—but how do you do that? You do that by taking the handcuffs

Predators players offer a stick salute to the fans. *Don Olea Photography.*

to seal the victory and give the Predators the opportunity to clinch a series on home ice—something they had never been given the chance to do in franchise history.

Holding a 3–2 lead late in game six, Anaheim was short handed with its goalie pulled. The puck found David Legwand's stick, and how fitting it was for Nashville's first-ever draft pick and all-time leading scorer to pot the empty net goal, clinching victory and securing the series in front of a raucous crowd at Bridgestone Arena.

"I could think of nothing else to say other than reference Rocky, and at the end of *Rocky II*, he goes, 'Yo Adrienne! I did it!'" said Pete Weber.

> *And I had to go, "Yo Adrienne, they did it! The Preds have won a round!"*
> *Now going on what turned out to be a fantastic series but coming up short against Vancouver. I'm never going to forget that series and going back and forth. I will never forget taking off from here after the Anaheim series was over and not knowing when we were going to start the series in Vancouver yet, so as we are landing, cell service begins to return to the phones, and we find out good thing we took off because the game was the next day!*

It was only a step in the right direction to the ultimate goal, but it was important to get the monkey off their back. Even though they would lose a

J.P. Dumont and Shane O'Brien celebrate a Predators goal. *Don Olea Photography*.

hard-fought series to the Vancouver Canucks in round two, the team had built tremendous momentum. It felt far removed from the days when rumors circulated about the moving. Acquiring Fisher was the centerpiece of the season that both Poile and Trotz thought put them over the edge in making the second round of the playoffs for the first time in franchise history.

"It was huge," said Barry Trotz.

I thought it was quite engaging. We were the better team who was more disciplined and stayed with it longer, and I thought the key move David made was acquiring Mike Fisher that year. He gave us a lot of belief and stability and a second line guy who could go against other people's top people on a day-to-day basis. It was huge; it was the elephant in the room. We'd made the playoffs a number of times, but we couldn't get by the first round.

In some of the early years, it was talent related where we were such big underdogs and we just didn't have enough talent. Then it went to we have enough talent, maybe we were a little bit smaller still, but we still got through. We got through on little-to-no health issues, but we just played a team who just played better…it was a little bit of an elephant in the room, and we got rid of it. The travel in that series was incredible. Winning was a breakthrough, and going against a good Vancouver team in a big Canadian market gave the Preds a lot of respect. It was the first time the Canadian market gave us the respect that was due.

"It's a steppingstone to get to the ultimate goal," said Poile.

As we know today, with the parity we have in this league, it is hard just to make the playoffs. When you get in the playoffs, you think you have a chance, but you have to have a little bit of success to believe that, and for a franchise, beating a team like Detroit a few years before and beating Anaheim, those are things that give you that confidence, that swagger to get you forward and compete for the Stanley Cup, which is what we are all in this game for.

GOING GOLD

Changes were not over yet. The summer of 2011 saw a rebranding of the Nashville Predators. In order to become a more distinctive brand and modernize the look of the team, Nashville went gold. The Predators logo was simplified to gold, blue and white. They also added a secondary logo, which feature the tri-star logo as seen on the Tennessee state flag but placed instead on a guitar pick. The new branding helped the team stand out from any other in the league. While the new logos sparked questions by some fans at the beginning, they have quickly grown on the fan base at large, and the amount of fans wearing jerseys at Bridgestone Arena has been widely noticed by not only locals but also Canadian media.

"That grand vision for the rebranding started before we even got here," said Sean Henry.

That was Tom Cigarran's idea. The one thing he said is that we are a unique team and we deserve our own identity; we deserve to have everyone, everyone, know when you see this, you know what team that fan loves. Then you start thinking of what does that mean. It was Tom's vision because we have so many jerseys, an evolution of them, in our conference room, and it's all over. The Yankees and Canadians have had basically one logo with minor tweaks. All the great logos that we talk about today are one hundred years old, but there's been a consistency. Tom said, "We start today with our consistency" wherever that meant, which was the strong logo that we have but simplified a bit and the bold, dominant single color. And that's what you have in gold. When you look across the spectrum at all teams in all sports, it's not used or has the fewest frequency of use. We can own it, and it can be our tradition. When we win, people remember that dominant color. There are so many teams with just pick your color. Too many with red, I think. We knew we'd start with that new jersey the following year. We were fortunate enough to catch a little magic in our first year in it. The previous year we make it to the second round for the first time, and the hints of gold were dropped pretty strongly with our rally towels and T-shirts. All of our ads were building toward that in a way. And again, we were fortunate that the players did what they did that year and allowed us to get into that second round to really have some fun with it, and it made it a little bit easier.

When the first one was leaked, it was a good thing. We weren't heartbroken that it was leaked because people hated it. It was a yellow-y cross between Michigan and Sweden jersey. Canary yellow. We got to say it wasn't it. Then, when we blew it out there and didn't know what people were going to say. Let's face it, no matter what you do, there's a percentage of people that aren't going to like it, and a certain amount that will like it no matter what. It's the ones in between that you have to worry about. Where are they going to fall? Let's get them around the people that love it a little bit more. That was the year we gave jerseys to full season ticket holders if they renewed by a certain date to kind of get it out there. People love the history of our jerseys. There are certain fans that have been here since day one that will always wear certain jerseys on certain days or against certain opponents, and that's great. But we also knew everything we did had to be gold. We had to bring new personality into the building. You come here for memories. Everything in the building was gray. There isn't any memory making with that. You could have been in Tacoma, Nashville or Boston, no idea where you were when you walked in our building. That's a mistake because so many great moments have happened here—CMAs, SEC tournament, Nashville Predators, concerts. We needed a theme. Concerts would be red and black, Bridgestone's colors. Hockey and sports are gold. Golden memories. There were so many natural things.

Then we wanted to add player personalities throughout the building. When we rolled it out, basically every week, two more columns were wrapped with player images. We knew our fans owned the team, but we wanted them to own the building and the experience because it's so unique. So you started seeing more gold in the building. Our team store converted to all gold. It was just a lot of fun. Then you get to the second round again, and we were fortunate enough to beat a team that was a big rival to us, with the Red Wings. It's easy to fall in love when winning happens. The funny thing is that when you watch an away game against St. Louis or Chicago and there are twenty of our fans there, you see them instantly. It stands out.

My son and I went to a Blackhawks game a couple years ago, and he's wearing his gold jersey. We're in their team store, nothing but red all the way around. I took a picture of him and showed it to Tom and said, "You were right, look at this." So that was kind of neat. You want to make it stand out, but more importantly, you want to make it your own. Right or wrong, there's one team that owns gold in all of sports, and it's us. That's pretty cool.

From then on, it was clear that the Predators were going to continue to paint the town gold.

"What are we known for? We're Music City," said Henry. "You have the piano keyboard in the collar, guitar strings across the numbers, all subtle. We didn't tell anyone about it. We wanted a unique uniform for a unique brand for a unique, passionate fan base. We should have the most passionate jerseys. Then you pick up the state logo and combine it with a guitar pick, and you have something pretty special."

It was the little things that made the jersey fairly popular. There was an essence of Nashville being incorporated without anything to make the jersey look touristy. Now, it's easy to spot a Predators fan among any crowd in the league.

Changes on the Bench

The new season also brought in a coaching change on the bench with Barry Trotz. With Brent Peterson battling Parkinson's disease, he stepped down to take a lighter role within the organization. Promoted to the role of assistant coach was Lane Lambert, who had been serving as head coach for the Milwaukee Admirals.

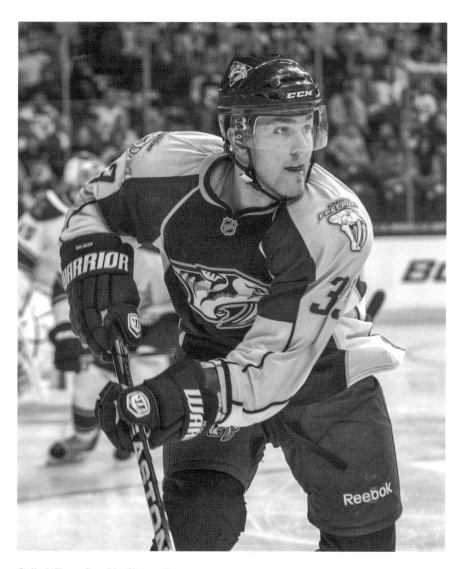

Colin Wilson. *Don Olea Photography*.

"It was a special year. I had just come off of a year where they had just won a playoff round, and then we ended up having a great season," said Lambert. "We went into the playoffs again and beat Detroit. Unfortunately, we didn't advance past the second round, but I think the good thing for me were those fun years in Milwaukee, and most of the players that were on that team I had coached in Milwaukee, so I got to see them grow and help them accomplish their goals as well."

One thing that helped Lambert in his transition was knowing multiple players on the roster for the Predators since he had coached them in Milwaukee. There were many players he knew had potential to be great.

"There were a number of guys at that time," said Lambert of players with high potential. "We had Colin Wilson, who was just starting out; Roman Josi, who was just starting out; Nick Spaling, [who] was a contributing player during that time; Pekka Rinne, obviously. I coached him for three years on that team, and he was at that point in time becoming the elite goaltender that he is. Regardless of what their role was, it was very gratifying to see them get to where they wanted to be."

The experience that Lambert gained in his three years with Barry Trotz in Nashville has helped him grow as a coach—so much that he went with Trotz to the Washington Capitals for the 2014–15 season.

Pekka Rinne stretches during a stoppage in play. *Christina McCullough.*

"I think for me, watching him on a day-to-day basis and seeing how he handles different situations has helped me," said Lambert of Trotz.

> *We have somewhat different personalities, and it has been a good learning experience to see what works from his standpoint. The other thing is he has given me the opportunity to coach without him being a micromanager. He hires people and lets them do their jobs, and as a result, I felt that I have been able to grow as a coach and develop things you may not be able to if you were working with a guy who didn't give you the same leisure.*

In his first season on the Nashville bench, Lambert was able to be a part of another successful season with Barry Trotz. The team would not only make the second round for the second year in a row, but it would also be playing against longtime rival Detroit Red Wings. Not only was the series victory against a divisional rival, but also the Predators took care of Detroit in just five games.

"That was a special time because the Detroit Red Wings were sort of the benchmark at that time and had been for quite a while," said Lambert.

> *I know in the early days there were a lot of Red Wings jerseys in the stands, and the tide had shifted. It was special to see the fans and the city and everyone who had been associated and involved with the team since day one. The last minute of the game was tense—they had pulled their goalie, and we were up by a goal—so by that point it was business as usual, but once the final buzzer went, we were able to enjoy it.*

As Nashville headed to the second round for the second straight year, it would face a hot goaltender in Mike Smith of the Phoenix Coyotes and lose the series 4-1. The series was not without its own drama, however. Prior to the trade deadline, the Predators acquired Andrei Kostitsyn from the Montreal Canadiens. His brother, Sergei Kostitsyn, was already a member of the team at the time. Near the end of the season, Alexander Radulov, the player who had jettisoned for the Kontinental Hockey League in Russia, made his return to the team just in time for the playoffs. While the team performed very well in round one against Detroit, the wheels came off against Phoenix.

Following a 5–3 loss in game two of the series, putting Nashville down 2-0, the Predators reported that both Andrei Kostitsyn and Alexander Radulov would be suspended from game three for violating team rules. While the exact story of what happened became a he said/she said, this was the beginning of the end for the team in that series. Nashville won game three at home, but it would be the only victory it would take during the series.

After the utter collapse following so much momentum, the NHL once again went through a work stoppage. The Predators had once again built on the success of the previous season only to have the beginning of the next season delayed. In addition, the 2012 offseason was one of heartbreak and disbelief as Ryan Suter left as an unrestricted free agent and captain Shea Weber signed an offer sheet with the Philadelphia Flyers, which the Predators obviously matched.

The drama from the previous playoffs, coupled with the free agency fiasco, did not help the stress levels of Nashville fans. If the season were delayed, it would only add to the stress. Unfortunately, the 2012–13 season turned into the 2013 season alone, as the first puck drop came on January 19, 2013. News broke of the lockout being lifted in the early morning hours of January 6, 2013. The NHL put together a forty-eight-game schedule to be played in just four months. It did not go well for the Predators as they finished last in the division and fourth to last in the league.

"I think everybody in the league was equally affected," said Pete Weber.

> *I don't think there were any signings that got held up; the team just did not come out well. That action was probably closer to the expansion sort of season that I had anticipated in the fall of 1998. I guess it showed that the team had to be re-tooled a little bit, and so two years later, ultimately, it was, but that was a crazy period of time. I had my iPad on in the middle of the night. I had gone to a restroom stop at the house, and I had read the news that the lockout looked like it was over, and I had to be so careful not to wake up Claudia, but that's the way I felt. I felt like going yipee-yo-yie-yay.*

If there was a bright spot for the poor finish in the 2013 season, it was that the Predators, for the first time since 2008, picked in the single digits of the first round of the draft. Not only that, but it was their second-highest pick ever. With the fourth overall pick in the 2013 draft, Nashville selected defenseman Seth Jones. Jones, who had recently come off a gold medal finish with Team USA in the World Junior Championship, was said to be the next franchise defenseman for whatever team drafted him. Lo and behold, a team known for developing excellent blue liners picked the next great American defenseman.

The next season was up and down the entire year for the team. At times, it remained competitive. At other times, it looked confused—all signs of some growing pains in giving younger players more of an opportunity. As Weber said, it took a bit of re-tooling on the part of Barry Trotz following the second-round loss in 2012 and the lockout-shortened season.

For the 2013–14 season, Nashville would close strong, going 7-1-2 in its last ten games, but it wasn't enough. The team finished just three points out of the last wild card spot for the playoffs. Most knew then that change was imminent.

6
A NEW ERA ON THE RISE

On April 14, 2014, the Nashville Predators parted ways with Barry Trotz, the only head coach the organization had ever known. It was an extremely emotional parting, but one that seemed mutual on both sides. After two seasons of missing the playoffs following two seasons of second-round appearances, the Predators decided to move on and not renew Trotz's contract. The contract, which was set to expire on June 30, 2014, was simply not going to be renewed. While the Predators did offer Trotz a position with hockey operations, he knew that he still had too much left to accomplish as a head coach.

Trotz left behind not only a plethora of memories but also a legacy as a figurehead of hockey in Nashville. Barry Trotz became the face of the organization over his tenure. He helped grow the game and teach fans the sport of hockey. He was highly involved in the community and always had time for fans. That's just Barry Trotz. His legacy will always live on, and as he's said, Nashville is home.

"I think what I would want it to be is that I am a builder," said Trotz of his legacy.

> I think I was a builder in hockey in Nashville with the Predators and David Poile. One of the things that was unique about Nashville is that there was stability. David has been there a long time; I was there a long time, and I became a face for a number of years with the franchise.
>
> My legacy is that, coming back to Nashville when I am retired and maybe with grandkids and watch[ing] NHL hockey in Nashville,

Tennessee, well, going back from the first couple years behind the scenes, where are we staying, where are we getting sold, are we moving, all of those things. It is pretty phenomenal to see that the Nashville Predators are very stable and successful as a part of a community in a solid way. There will be hockey there for another one hundred years—that is the legacy I would like to leave...I was one of the people who brought hockey to Nashville by being a constant in the hockey circle or the community circle for Nashville, and they are taking action.

One of the first things Craig Leipold asked was we are going to have to work hard to become Nashville's team so we would need someone in the community and teaching the game, and I think everyone in the organization accomplished that through the hard years when the building wasn't full and we didn't have great teams and other threats of us moving and therefore the local sponsorship was "Are we in or are we out? I am not going to invest if they talk about moving." So it became hard to sell that, but at the same time we wanted to be successful, and for a team that wasn't so great, we were pretty successful at getting the most out of the players and resources given to us at that time.

We became a model for how to develop and draft and run an organization from a functionality standpoint where other teams can look at the Preds and say, "How can they have so much success when we have so many more resources, why are they having more success than us?" That is the consistent success we had. We didn't win a cup, but we were pretty successful in everybody else's mind around the league for being great competitors and finding ways to put a competitive product on the ice year in and year out.

Trotz's legacy will live on not just in Nashville but also in the hockey community in general. While he's moved on to a different venture, the fact remains that he was and still is an important part of the community. Anyone who ever spoke with Trotz knew that he was sincere. He truly has a connection with Nashville and Predators fans. Trotz is well liked by everyone he meets. It's a sign that not only was he the right coach at the right time for the Nashville Predators, but he was also the right man to help guide Nashville into becoming a legitimate hockey town.

"He was probably the most underrated coach for about ten years in this league until people realized just how good of a coach he was and how good his systems were able to work," said Craig Leipold.

New players would come in, but everyone would play the Nashville Predators system. No one ever wanted to play Nashville, and that was because of Barry and what he had done. Everybody who ever played for Barry, when they left the team would have tremendous respect for him. Not just as a coach but as a mentor, friend and a person they could trust. He is the real deal. When you meet Barry, you know Barry; there is no fake side to him. He is the person that, when he says he is going to do something, he does it. He works hard, and we were so lucky to have someone like him that fit so well into the culture of the Nashville community. It was one of those hires that worked out incredibly well.

When it was announced that Trotz's contract would not be extended, it was an emotional breakup. You can tell the impact a person has on others by how they say goodbye. At the closing of his emotional, tear-filled press conference, it was easy to see the relationship that Trotz had built not only with employees of the organization but also with members of the media. It's not often that a former head coach will stay and shake the hand of every media member seeking a handshake. Trotz did. He had personal conversations with anyone who wished to have one. That's just Barry Trotz. He truly cares about people and the relationships he has built. It's why he will always be beloved in Nashville.

THE LAVIOLETTE ERA BEGINS

It did not take long for the Nashville Predators to find the second head coach in their history. It had long been rumored that former Philadelphia Flyers head coach Peter Laviolette was the front-runner for the job thanks to his relationship with David Poile while working for Team USA during the World Championships. On May 6, 2014, Nashville made it official and hired Peter Laviolette as its next coach.

Before coming to Nashville, Peter Laviolette had experienced tremendous success in his previous positions. For his first two seasons as a head coach with the New York Islands, they made it to the playoffs. Laviolette then went on to win the Stanley Cup with the Carolina Hurricanes in 2006, which was his first full season with the team. When Laviolette moved on to the Philadelphia Flyers, he took over at the helm in the first third of the season and led the team to a loss in the Stanley Cup final. The Flyers reached the second round the following two season. Only three games into the 2013–14 season, Philadelphia terminated

Laviolette, and he became one of the most sought-after coaches the following off-season.

General manager David Poile thought all along that the organization was not in a true rebuilding mode and that the team had the necessary pieces to be successful immediately.

"I really felt that we weren't in a rebuilding situation," he said.

> *I thought we built the team up the past two years even though we didn't make the playoffs, and I quickly felt that I wanted to have a more veteran coach, and I certainly wanted to have a coach that played a different style than Barry. And that is no disrespect to Barry, but if we're going to make a change, let's make a change.*
>
> *I had known Peter from before working with him during the Olympics and a little bit of the stuff for Team USA, and when he came in to interview, all the things he said were exactly what I wanted to hear. Checking with the people he had worked with or for and how he coached and what the results were in the first year taking on playoff teams, it was a perfect fit for what we needed.*

It was a mutual need fulfilled for both the organization and Peter Laviolette. Each thought it was a perfect fit.

"I got to work with David Poile with the United States team and even the start of the World Championship team when Barry was still working here," said Laviolette.

> *Nashville had a lot of good pieces in place. It reminded me of a market like North Carolina, where my wife and I had already been and really enjoyed. To be honest, it was an opportunity to coach again. When you are sitting out and you get an opportunity and someone is interested in you, there are not a lot of NHL coaching jobs available. I was grateful for the opportunity that David offered me. There are a lot of positives with my recollection of Nashville—the fans, the building and knowing some of the players in the lineup.*

Already being one month behind into the off-season, the Predators had a lot of work to do not only to prepare for the draft but also for free agency so the new head coach could begin to build the team the way he wanted it.

"The one thing I wanted to establish was the way we were going to play the game. I wanted us to have an identity that people were going to see when they watched the game," said Laviolette.

James Neal. *Christina McCullough.*

They would be able to see the passion, the attack, the forward motion of how we were going to play. We worked on it from day one, and I do think we accomplished that. I think we changed the way we wanted to play. I think that led us to success.

The other thing I noticed from day one was how effective the leadership group was. When you come into a team and you start to practice and do work on the ice, I think your veteran players are the ones working hardest and buying into it the most. Guys like Shea Weber, Pekka Rinne, Mike Fisher, James Neal, Paul Gaustad and Eric Nystrom are excellent leaders. They lead by example, and they go out there and do what they did in practice from day one in training camp. We had a good start to the season.

Having a core leadership group already in place certainly helped the 2014–15 Nashville Predators. The team had one of its most successful seasons in history in the first season with Peter Laviolette at the helm.

But before the season began, David Poile had executed a trade at the 2014 NHL Entry Draft that sent shockwaves through the fan base and the hockey world in general. Highly considered more of a hockey trade than anything else, Poile sent Patric Hornqvist and, at the time, upcoming restricted free agent Nick Spaling to the Pittsburgh Penguins in exchange for known sniper James Neal. Overall, the trade proved beneficial for each team. Poile wanted to add a little more excitement to the roster with the trade.

"We were looking for a bang and to bring to the players' attention that how we played the last few years wasn't good enough and to make a statement that we are in it to make the playoffs and make them to go further," said Poile. "So James Neal, coaching change, six or seven forwards overall were changed so there were a lot of changes in the off-season, so when you come into training camp you know it's going to be different. Will we win? I don't know, but it's going to be different."

At many points during the season, the team held on to the first overall position in the league. The team would finish with a 47-25-10, good enough for 104 points and second in the Central Division. Even though the team ended up losing to the eventual Stanley Cup champion Chicago Blackhawks in the first round, the first season under Laviolette proved to be exciting and reenergized the fan base.

"What Peter brought was the idea that you have to do everything you can to cultivate offensive creativity, and if it takes absorbing a few bad cross-ice passes and turning them into one-on-ones or three-on-twos, he's going to do it," said Pete Weber. "Colin Wilson, perhaps more than anybody else, benefited from that approach. What we have seen him do is he has plans for what you do all the time in attacking zone, not just the D-zone, and I think that's something that will permeate hockey more and more now, particularly as we've watched the playoffs this spring and early summer, you can see how darn difficult it is to score goals."

Before the 2014–15 season began, David Poile made it known that the expectation and goal was to make the playoffs. With the regular season performance, that certainly changed as the fans expected more of a championship run compared to just making it to the playoffs. That being said, the season was still a good step in the right direction.

"I think making the playoffs was a great first step. It was a terrible feeling the past two years not to make the playoffs," said Poile.

> *We all know we are going to be judged for what we do in the playoffs, whether it's this year or next year. Can't go too far. You have to have some success as a team and as a management group and a coaching staff, and if you don't, changes are going to be made. It's hard to keep the team the same, and there is no time better in the present than the way we played this year for the most part. We know we can beat any team on any given night, but we can struggle and lose on any given night, so that is all part of what we are looking forward to…is how we play in the playoffs because deep down I think we feel we have a really good chance to be successful.*

One of the players that truly helped in the success of Peter Laviolette's first season was rookie sensation Filip Forsberg. Forsberg was acquired by trade with the Washington Capitals on April 3, 2013. The trade, which sent Martin Erat and Michael Latta to the Capitals in exchange for Forsberg, the eleventh overall pick in the 2012 NHL Entry Draft, is already considered a tremendous win for the Predators. Easily so, in that during his first full NHL season, Forsberg generated sixty-three points (twenty-six goals, thirty-seven assists), good enough to be the leading scorer on the team in the regular season. Forsberg credited much of his success to spending time with American Hockey League affiliate the Milwaukee Admirals. He also knows consistency will be important for continued success.

"I got more comfortable playing on the smaller ice surface and the North American type of hockey, and I think it was a good year learning wise," said Forsberg. "The key is to stay consistent and keep trying to get better for every

Filip Forsberg. *Christina McCullough.*

day. The NHL is so tough these days, so it really takes a lot of work to be successful, and that's the biggest key for me in the future."

Forward Craig Smith has also seen success in his young career in Nashville. In his first season under Peter Laviolette, Smith spent time between the first and second lines, surrounded by talent. He put up his second-best season points-wise but was always a threat on the ice.

"I think it comes a lot with our ability; he played to our strengths," said Smith on Laviolette's coaching style. "We have a lot of guys that are hardworking, great skating players, and he adapted to that, too. He used what we had, and we were committed to success from there. I think his tenacity and aggressive style is only going to help us. I think we attached to it, and that is how we like to play, so it's a great fit."

The 2014–15 season was one of adaptation and success for both players and coaches. Players had to adjust to a different coaching style. Peter Laviolette had to get acquainted with a new city and a new team. Establishing himself in the community was a role that Laviolette knew would be important, and it was one that he looked forward to when he moved to Nashville.

"I think the nontraditional markets have a little bit more of a connection between the fans and the community in regards to the players and the

Above: Craig Smith. *Christina McCullough*.

Right: Weber and teammates celebrate a Nashville goal. *Christina McCullough*.

coaches because it is something that is built internally between both," said Laviolette.

> There is a relationship that forms there with regard to our fans, and it is just amazing for me to watch how this unfolded and for the life to come back into the Predators and the building and the organization this year. It started going right from the start. We were successful right from the beginning, and we started to grow and build. There was a really positive buzz about the team this year.
>
> The work that the players do in the community in regard to schools, the 365 Fund, the charities and the way they go out and help is just amazing. You see the wives and what they are able to do in different situations, as well. So much good can come from an organization.

With the success of the most recent season and the ability to compete with the league's best teams, the Predators are proving that they are long gone from the days when it was feared the team might move. Former television color analyst and Stanley Cup winner Terry Crisp understands how important momentum and stability are for a franchise.

"It's a combination of everything," said Crisp.

> A stable ownership, which we definitely have right now, with one intent to keep this team in this city and to make this city grow. You've got the Titans, an NHL team, the Sounds [MiLB] going strong, and that was their main objective. That, to me, is a solid sign, and then as the expectations started to grow for the fans, boy you're coming around when they can tell you what's wrong and they aren't guessing, they're telling you the truth. We have a good young core, a few little tweaks here and there, and I feel like we could have beat Chicago this year. In other years, you're not too sure, but to me that's a sign we've arrived. Everyone was upset this year— fans, players, managers—that we didn't beat Chicago.

It's a good problem for a franchise to have when expectations continue to rise. When fans and players alike begin to expect championships in the near future, it shows just how far the franchise has come. Attendance numbers are strong, and in the 2014–15 season, the Nashville Predators set a franchise record of thirty sellouts. On December 14, 2014, the Predators set an attendance record against the St. Louis Blues when attendance topped 17,401 (official capacity is set at 17,113, according to the predators.nhl.com).

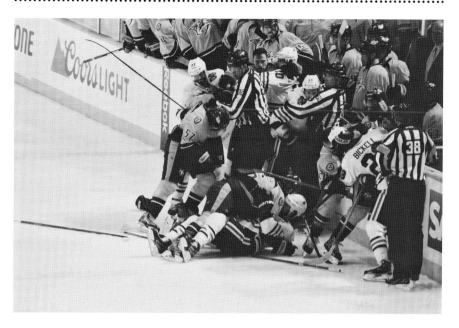

A fracas ensues during game two of the first round of the 2015 Stanley Cup playoffs between the Predators and Blackhawks. *Christina McCullough.*

As the Predators continue to see success, hockey will continue to see success in the South. With the Atlanta Thrashers now playing as the Winnipeg Jets, the reach for Nashville goes from Kentucky to Alabama and Georgia. All are places that continue to grow, with an NCAA Division I college hockey team in Huntsville, non-varsity college hockey teams in each state, travel teams and high school hockey. It can only go up from here.

7
GROWING UP HOCKEY

It takes a generation for a market to develop and ingrain itself in a community. That's exactly what has happened with the Predators. After being around for seventeen-plus years, it is finally coming full circle to where children who used to attend games with their parents in the early years are now finally old enough to purchase ticket packages for themselves. There are now diehard fans who have grown up not knowing what it's like to be in a city without a professional hockey team.

"Once they got their team, you had a hardcore bunch of fans here that were bound and determined this team would stay here, along with some good ownership who put their own money on the line and decided we were going to keep it," said Terry Crisp.

The fans here were dedicated whether it was four thousand, five thousand, six thousand—they were here hardcore, and that is what made this team. Then they grew, and we started Hockey 101. Pete and I used to do them three or four times a week, and it was hilarious. We should have taped it all for the questions they asked and the things that we told them and talked to them about. We'd tell them about icing then go on the air and say what icing was, and the people just grew with it.

Now we are getting all of that coming back home. When we started out, kids that were born then are now seventeen years old. We are starting to reap the benefits of those fans bringing their kids, and now you see minor hockey, high school hockey, a men's league—there are a dozen or more in the city that weren't here before. What amazes me is the growth in seventeen years. It makes you proud to be part of this. Anyone who comes here—from Europe or Canada, anywhere—comes to a game here, and not once have I not heard them leave here and say what a fun game that was. Not if we won or lost, not what the scoreboard was, but what a great evening, we were entertained, the whole atmosphere here is happening.

Over the past few years, the youth and adult hockey numbers have boomed in Music City. USA Hockey registrations continue to grow, and some say that Nashville is on the brink of becoming a hockey hotbed for producing NHL-caliber players.

"I think the quality of the players, the quality of the coaching—what I found is that the coaches who are involved in hockey are very passionate and on the next level of coaching techniques," said Barry Trotz.

I think there is a group of kids now that are looking at the Shea Webers and Roman Josis and all the people coming through, and they love the game and are taking it more seriously, and the better athletes starting playing it. I think high school hockey has a big effect on that, and obviously the Preds did because they got young kids in the learn-to-skate program, and the parents go to games and like it, and people grew from that. Lo and behold, a lot of players are coming out of that.

When some high school teams first started, schools had to be combined to compete. While some still share teams, the growth of high school hockey has become so great in Middle Tennessee that multiple teams have now made it to national competitions. Youth hockey teams from Nashville travel to Canada and win. Travel teams go to "traditional" areas for the sport and win. Nashville is proving that just because the players are from the South, it doesn't mean that they can't go up north and win.

From 2002–03 to 2012–13, USA Hockey numbers for Tennessee grew by 43.1 percent. Now, with the addition of Ford Ice Center, new hockey players are signing up almost every day. The demand is there for more ice already, as adult and youth hockey programs are reaching their limits in a facility that is only one year old. It's not just Tennessee, however. Areas all around the Sunbelt are experiencing tremendous hockey growth, and it deserves to be talked about.

"I believe when we came here in the fall of '98, there were less than three hundred registered amateur players, and now it's up about tenfold," said Pete Weber.

Nashville Predators captain Shea Weber. *Kristen Jerkins.*

I think three high schools were playing the game as clubs, and now there are about twenty clubs representing high schools. We have more ice surfaces—that is an incredible thing—so it's not just on Thursday and Saturday nights in this building, it's at A-Game, it's at Ford Ice Center, it's at Centennial. I think the one thing I should have advised everybody was to buy stock in Febreze because mothers need that for those smelly bags that they have to put up in the back of their SUVs when they get home. They are putting Division I hockey at Arizona State coming up this year. I think UCLA will probably be next because of my friends out there, so that has been tremendous to watch.

All of this couldn't have been done without building more ice around the Nashville area. From the instant Jeff Cogen and Sean Henry arrived, they knew that expanding the amount of rinks in the area was a necessity. It had been done in both of their previous communities, and it helped grow the game immensely. Thus, Ford Ice Center went from an idea to a reality very quickly.

"Well it's simple," said Henry.

You look at Dallas—before Minnesota even moved down, part of the deal was that they're investing in communities. From day one, you're introducing a great game, and this is how you can play and infiltrate the whole area. That didn't happen here. When the team came, it was a great game, but it was hard to grow youth hockey. Barry Trotz, Brent Peterson, David Poile, our training staff, half the employees here came from somewhere with a hockey background. There were rinks in malls, at schools, everywhere. They were putting sticks in kids' hands, but there wasn't enough ice. At some point, kids want to emulate the guys they love. Sure, street hockey is a great game, but it's reinforced by playing on ice. The game is for everybody. There's just something unique about wearing your team's jersey while doing their sport the way they do it on the ice. So one of the very first things that we did is that we were very fortunate in partner[ing] with Mayor Dean, Greg Hinote and Rich Riebeling. We were very aggressive with them and had an opportunity with the new lease to do it together. Even better, they jumped on it.

The really neat thing is that we were excited about where we put it in Antioch—an area where the mall was basically vacant, save for a few tenants. We put it in an area that needed a shot in the arm and, for whatever reason, was going in the wrong way for many years. It was just coming out of that, but no one knew about it. Before we built Ford Ice, it was starting to head in the right direction after so many years in the wrong way. So when we had the opportunity, we were pretty excited about it. We knew what would happen. It would just blow up and bring new people there. A lot of people got the opportunity to reintroduce themselves to Antioch or discover it for the first time through hockey. So that public/private partnership with the library, the rec center and the park, we knew when that's successful, we can take that model and replicate it, maybe in Davidson County, maybe in adjoining counties. We're going to have these concentric circles. People get mad at me when I say what I'm about to say, but we need six, seven, eight, nine of those centers in the area. Look at like north, south, central, east, west. Once we have that, we expand beyond that. And we're going to get that done because of the success of Ford Ice and what it's done for that community, what it's done for the branding and reintroduction of Antioch.

Then you look at what it's done on the ice, and that's critical. Building these two extra sheets of ice will make all of us, Centennial Sportsplex and A-Game Sportsplex, busier. It's just that simple. If we don't increase USA Hockey registrations, we all fail, so let's do it together. Let's have a unified approach to it. They did it with us. The end result, in less than a year, we've increased USA Hockey registrations by over 35 percent. So in less than a year, we didn't just replace what we're taking, if you will; we *have more registered USA Hockey participants per rink than we did just a year ago. It's successful, and we're just starting to see the glimpse of it. The Scott Hamilton Skating School allows people to learn to skate at any age and have fun with it. In the end, we just want people to fall in love with being a little bit cold and skating around. We couldn't be happier with it, and the best is yet to come at Ford Ice.*

College hockey is making itself known not just in the Nashville area but also in the entire Southeast region. Vanderbilt University has become a staple tenant at Ford Ice Center. Along with Vanderbilt, Middle Tennessee State University has been able to make a resurgence in its hockey program. Other schools like Sewanee: The University of the South; Trevecca Nazarene University; Belmont University; and Lipscomb University are all making progress in icing teams. Outside Nashville, other teams known for being in the Southeastern Conference in other sports are making their way into hockey. The University of Alabama and University of Arkansas have both moved up to play Division I non-varsity hockey, just one step away from being a varsity sport.

Just under two hours away to the south of Nashville is Huntsville, Alabama. Not only is Huntsville home to a hockey team that has won multiple national championships, but it's also home to the only NCAA Division I college hockey team in the South in the University of Alabama–Huntsville Chargers. Since 1985, hockey has been a varsity sport at UAH and an NCAA sport since 1986. The squad has also produced two NHL players in Jared Ross (Philadelphia Flyers, 2008–10) and Cam Talbot (New York Rangers, 2013–15; and Edmonton Oilers, 2015–present).

While the Chargers have been in existence much longer than the Predators, the influence of an NHL team can be felt in Huntsville. Television broadcasts for the Predators reach from Alabama to Georgia and north into Kentucky. Recruiting for UAH is heavy on local players, many of them now growing up as fans of the Predators.

The question isn't asked nearly as much as it was just five years ago. Is Nashville a hockey market? Some still question it, but those who have experienced a game at Bridgestone Arena will never ask it again.

"When I heard the fans yell, 'Refs you suck!' now we're coming of age, now we're in the hockey world," said Crisp.

Probably when the fans were upset when we made the playoffs and lost, that was a good sign. We made it and worked so hard, and we're out the first round. It wasn't like, oh, this is nice we made the playoffs; they were upset. They were mad that we didn't go a little further, and that is a sign they are growing up, a sign they were past the fact that we played well and the fact we won certain games and beat certain teams along the way, but that we wanted more.

Craig Smith grew up in Wisconsin, obviously surrounded by hockey. When he first started in Nashville, he didn't know what to expect. It soon became apparent that the fans not only knew the game but were also passionate about it.

"I had no idea when I got here, at the games on Tuesday and Thursday nights, you don't know what to expect and you are getting packed houses," said Smith. "It was loud as any building in the league, and it makes it a lot of fun. The fans are committed, and they love watching us."

It's easy to see how Nashville is a hockey market, but when will it know when it has made it? When it can never be questioned again by some elitists? Sean Henry has the right thought behind it.

"I remember I was with Phil Esposito in Florida and someone asked him the question of when will we know when we've made it in Florida," said Henry.

And he said, "Not when you think. Not when we've won a Stanley Cup. Not when people aren't questioning whether we should have a team or not, but when kids get drafted on a regular basis that were born here, learned to skate here and could stay here through competitive hockey and into college. Until that happens, we haven't made it." When I got here, obviously we had Blake Geoffrion drafted. He grew up here and started playing hockey here, obviously excelled quickly but had to leave at a young age to continue his competitive hockey. So we can claim him, but in reality, that's when I think we're going to make it. When is that going to be? I think there are probably a few kids playing right now, whether it's a six- or fourteen-year-old, that could make it. We're getting closer. With the Elite Edge Hockey Showcase, players getting drafted into junior hockey, players going to play college hockey. I think it's sooner when we think. When will someone start skating in Antioch, which opened a year ago? Maybe we're eight years away.

As Nashville prepares to host the 2016 NHL All-Star Game, it's almost come full circle since the last league-wide event was held in the city. The 2003 NHL Entry Draft saw captain Shea Weber drafted in Nashville. Now,

Black Geoffrion gives LA Kings captain Dustin Brown a friendly shove. *Don Olea Photography.*

all things considered, he'll be able to defend his hardest shot in the city where he was drafted. The team and city will be in the limelight for not just the league but also the entire hockey world. You can rest assured that they will make it an event to be remembered.

At activities for the All-Star Game, there will be many children, youth hockey players, kids who dream of playing the game. Who knows, there may just be a future NHL star in the stands watching a favorite player take the ice. It has been seen so much now, with players being drafted out of countries like Australia and China, as well as Southern California, Texas and even Tennessee (with Blake Geoffrion), that there are hockey players all over this world. They just have to be introduced to the game to give them a chance to fall in love with it.

SELECTED BIBLIOGRAPHY

Ford Ice Center. "The Official Web Site—Ford Ice Center." June 13, 2015. Fordicecenter.com (accessed June 14, 2015).

Nashville Predators. "Nashville Predators." May 20, 2013. http://predators.nhl.com (accessed May 19, 2015).

Peters, Chris. "U.S. Hockey Participation Numbers for 2013–14." The United States of Hockey, June 17, 2014. Unitedstatesofhockey.com (accessed June 19, 2015).

2014–15 Division Standings. "Schedule." May 20, 2015. http://predators.nhl.com/club/standings.htm (accessed June 16, 2015).

Witman, Alexis. "By the Numbers: Preds Statistics of Note in 2014–15." Nashville Predators, April 9, 2015. http://predators.nhl.com/club/news.htm?id=762320 (accessed May 9, 2015).

INDEX

INDEX

ABOUT THE AUTHOR

Justin Bradford is the managing editor, lead writer and host of *Penalty Box Radio* as heard on 102.5 The Game ESPN Nashville. Born in Michigan, he moved to Tennessee when he was only seven years old. A child of the General Motors relocation, his roots were in Michigan, but he has assimilated to Tennessee over time.

Bradford has been a hockey fan for his entire life, Steve Yzerman being his hockey idol. Don't fear, Predators fans, Bradford changed allegiances upon the inception the Predators organization. Upon graduating college, he quickly became a season ticket holder in the infamous Cell Block, Section 303. That's where his super fandom was born.

In 2012, he and Ben Butzbach started *Penalty Box Radio*, a show and site that would not only cover the Nashville Predators but also feature stories on prospects and junior and college hockey. Both the show and the site took off. Both Bradford and *Penalty Box Radio* have won Toast of Music City Awards. In 2013, Bradford placed second in the Best Sports Report category. In 2014, Bradford won the Best Sports Reporter award, and "Penalty Box Radio" was voted the second-best blog in Nashville. Not only does *Penalty*

Box Radio cover the Predators, but it's also the radio home of the Nashville Junior Predators and Vanderbilt Hockey.

Hockey has been a huge part of Bradford's life. Vacations are usually spent traveling to cover hockey games. His travels have taken him all over Ontario and British Columbia, as well as Raleigh and Dallas—all for the love of hockey.